ATLAS *of* IRISH HISTORY

Third Edition

D1344131

ATLAS *of* IRISH HISTORY

Third Edition

Seán Duffy

Gabriel Doherty

Raymond Gillespie

James Kelly

Colm Lennon

Brendan Smith

GILL BOOKS

Gill Books
Hume Avenue, Park West, Dublin 12
www.gillbooks.ie

Gill Books is an imprint of M.H. Gill & Co.

© 1997, 2000, 2011, 2012 Arcadia Editions Limited
Derbyshire, England
978 07171 5399 2

First hardback edition published in 1997; second edition
in 2000; third edition in 2011. This paperback edition
first published in 2012

Printed in Italy by Printer Trento S.r.l.

A CIP catalogue record for this book is available
from the British Library.

10 9 8 7 6

Contributors

Seán Duffy is Associate Professor of Medieval History in Trinity College, Dublin.

Gabriel Doherty teaches in the Department of History, University College, Cork.

Raymond Gillespie teaches in the Department of History at St Patrick's College, Maynooth.

James Kelly teaches in the Department of History at St Patrick's College, Drumcondra, Dublin.

Colm Lennon is a former lecturer in the Department of History at St Patrick's College, Maynooth.

Brendan Smith teaches history in the Department of Historical Studies at the University of Bristol.

Contents

Foreword

OUT ON THE WESTERN EDGE of Europe, a first glance at the map makes Ireland seem a small and isolated place. However, many peoples have by turns established themselves on this remote island, creating an historical dynamic whose dispersed voices are now heard in almost every major city of the globe, in accents unmistakably from Cork or Connemara, Donegal or Dublin. This atlas attempts to explain in a visual, accessible way Ireland's unfolding story, and how this small country's remarkable worldwide impact has come about.

Some ten millennia ago, the first people arrived in Ireland, perhaps across the land bridge that once linked Ireland to Scotland, and began the region's human story. Not much more than two millennia ago arrived the ancestors of the Gaels, who after hundreds of years of assimilation and adaptation gave and continue to give the island its distinct identity.

Over the past thousand years, the Vikings, Normans, English and Scots have all left their mark on Ireland's culture, religion, language and landscape. They have also left schisms which survive to this day. For more than 800 years, Ireland's history was by degrees tied to that of England, moving from the margins of English royal interest to the status of a colony. From 1800 the island was governed directly from Westminster, with Irish soldiers guarding the Asian frontiers of Britain's global empire, Irish workers building bridges in Africa, and Irish settlers roaming the Canadian prairies. While the Irishman's wanderlust has never been in doubt, not all of this dispersion, however, was of Ireland's choosing.

Ireland's desire to set its own direction surfaced many times, and by the 1920s most of the island had secured its independence, with the exception of the north-east corner which remained within the United Kingdom. This partition, and its ramifications for both the southern state and Great Britain, continue to be hotly contested and debated, although the peace process has taken the worst of the heat out of the discussion.

The maps and texts of this atlas are intended to spotlight the movements of Ireland's long and multi-layered history and to explain how its present circumstances have arisen. Maps tend to show facts rather than influences or ideas, and as such are simply snapshots in time. This collection, however, is accompanied by text written by some of the leading authorities in the field, and it is hoped that, together, these contributions will go some way to explain the story of this unique and fascinating place.

For the authors

PART I: ORIGINS

Seán Duffy

FAINT TRACES of human food-gathering and hunting survive in Ireland from the Mesolithic period (perhaps as early as 8,000 BC). These early people may have migrated from Britain though hardly before the land-bridge between the islands was washed away, and such weapons and tools as they have left behind are mostly small flint blades. They lived on wild pig, small mammals, fowl, fish and edible plants, and dwelt in small huts in isolated bands and hunting-camps, perhaps migrating seasonally. The island must have been sparsely inhabited, and has yielded no evidence of artistic activity, or of agriculture.

Above: The chamber of the passage tomb at Newgrange, Co. Meath. The massive uprights are parts of the estimated 200,000 tonnes of stones transported to the site during its construction.

Ireland's first crop-growers and live-stock-breeders were Neolithic peoples who arrived by sea from Britain or the continent about 6,000 years ago. It was they who made the first real impact on Ireland's landscape, building more substantial houses and stone boundary walls. Their pottery and decoration developed, and there is evidence of 'industrial' activity in the form of the large-scale manufacture of axes. They also constructed numerous megalithic monuments such as passage-tombs, court-cairns and dolmens, used for burial and for ritualistic and cultic purposes. These are among the earliest examples of true architecture known anywhere in the world and many survive in the Irish landscape today, some preserving examples of advanced mural art.

During the Bronze Age (*c.* 2,500–600 BC) Ireland's first metal-workers, not necessarily new immigrants, exploited the island's rich copper deposits to produce copper and bronze axe- and spear-heads, and later, shields, cauldrons, sickles and craftsmen's tools. Their legacy includes beautiful personal ornaments, many in gold, such as earrings, fibulae (dress fasteners) and lunulae (an item of neck or hair jewellery, shaped like a half-moon). Later they produced a great variety of highly accomplished neck, arm and waist ornaments, the pre-historic goldsmiths' craft probably reaching its peak at about 700 BC. In fact, more gold-crafted objects survive from this period in Ireland than in any other country in western or northern Europe, and some objects of Irish type have been found in Britain and the continent, suggesting an active export trade. From this period, too, may belong the many stone circles and 'wedge' tombs throughout the countryside. Pottery used for food and funerary urns also reached a high standard.

By about 600 BC iron had come to replace bronze as the main source-material for weapons and tools, and it was during the ensuing Iron Age that the first

Celtic peoples appeared in Ireland. They have left us the Irish language and art-work in the La Tène style associated with the Celts of central Europe. By the beginning of this period great hilltop enclosures like Tara and Emain Macha were in use, sites which sometimes also had an earlier importance. Though evidence is scanty, some cliff-top 'promontory forts' may date from this era, as may some 'crannóg' lake-dwellings. The Roman invasion of Britain affected Ireland to the extent that trading contacts with the Empire were enhanced, and Ireland may have provided a haven for refugees from the conquest, and a base from which to raid western Britain. As the Roman Empire declined, unrelated Irish colonies took root in what are now Wales and Cornwall and in western Scotland, the last being ultimately of greatest influence. It was probably in this period that the 'ring-fort' became established as the home of wealthy farmers, those with earthen banks usually being called 'raths' and those with stone walls, 'cashels'. Thousands of these still dot the countryside and many remained in use well into the historic period.

The historic period begins with the introduction of Christianity in the 5th century, and Ireland first emerges into the light of history in documents ascribed to the British missionary, St Patrick. Thereafter it developed a highly literate society which has left a substantial corpus of literature in both Latin and Irish, allowing us to form a mental picture of Dark-Age Ireland that is clearer and far more detailed than that offered by most other European countries. Using annals, genealogies, king-lists and other sources, we can assemble the names of the many peoples who dominated the island, the territories they held, and the rise and fall of their various dynasties. Other sources allow us to plot the progress of Christianity in the country, in which, by the mid-6th century, monks and monasteries had eclipsed bishops and dioceses, their houses becoming centres not just of piety, but of learning, study and art. The members of the monastic communities studied the Bible, the writings of the early Church Fathers, canon law and Latin grammar. They copied manuscripts, many of them beautifully illuminated, and commissioned masterpieces of metalwork and carved stone. As the monastic ideal flourished, earning Ireland the name 'island of saints', their missionaries spread to Britain and the continent, followed by scholars and teachers in what was truly a 'Golden Age'.

The 7th- and 8th-century law tracts, heavily influenced by the Scriptures, portray a society that was intensely hierarchical, where status and honour meant much, and where sharp distinctions were drawn between those regarded as 'sacred' (including kings, clerics and poets) and those who were not, and between the free and the unfree. On the highest rungs of the ladder stood the kings, around whom society revolved. Ireland was a land of many kings, the tracts defining three grades: kings of petty local kingdoms, over-kings ruling several of these, and 'kings of over-kings' who effectively ruled a whole province. Although the laws rarely refer to a high-king of all Ireland, it is clear that for much of the early historic period the leading dynasty, the Uí Néill who were based in the northern half of the country with their ceremonial capital at Tara, did claim, and were occasionally able to enforce, supremacy throughout the island. Their primacy was shattered in the early 11th century, and power then revolved around a half-dozen or so leading province-kings, each of whom sought to force his rivals into submission and make himself high-king.

It is difficult to assess the extent to which these changes were the result of the Viking incursions, which for a time in the 9th century appeared likely to overwhelm the country. The Vikings certainly increased the intensity of warfare in an already violent society, and by developing towns at Dublin, Waterford, Limerick, Wexford and Cork, and trading networks overseas, they added to the wealth of what was otherwise a largely pastoral economy. Their presence in strength in Munster no doubt contributed also to the decline of its reigning dynasty, the Eóganachta, and facilitated the rise of Brian Boru. His later fame was attributed to a notable victory over the Vikings at the Battle of Clontarf in 1014, but his real importance lies in the fact that he ended the monopoly on the high-kingship formerly held by the Uí Néill.

In time, the Viking enclaves were assimilated into the Irish political superstructure, and those Irish kings who succeeded in dominating them, in some cases establishing the Viking town as their capital, gained an advantage over their rivals in the race for the high-kingship. This was especially true in the case of Dublin, overlordship of which was by the late 10th century generally asserted by successful claimants to the high-kingship and which, by the mid-11th century, was directly ruled by Irish kings, effectively becoming the country's capital.

This period saw rapid changes in Ireland in both Church and state. The Gregorian reform movement, which sought to eradicate abuses in the Church throughout western Christendom, spread to Ireland by the early 12th century and, under the patronage of reform-minded Irish province-kings, was responsible for major changes in the organization of the Irish Church, though it was considerably less successful in eradicating abuses in Church practice and moral laxities among the laity. In secular affairs, the same period witnessed what may have been the evolution of a national monarchy, as a series of ambitious province-kings steadily increased their powers, started to act as feudal lords in the European mode, and sought to stamp their authority throughout the island. This, however, was cut short in the late 12th century by the Anglo-Norman invasion, spearheaded by men from the Welsh borderlands. They came at the instigation of the Leinster king, Diarmait MacMurchada (Dermot MacMurrough), who had been expelled by the reigning high-king, Ruaidrí Ua Conchobair (Rory O'Connor). The invaders were led by Richard de Clare, better known as Strongbow, who married MacMurchada's daughter and later succeeded to Leinster. At this point, late in 1171, Henry II, who had earlier received a papal licence to invade Ireland in order, it was claimed, to aid in the process of Church reform, came to Ireland himself, the first English king ever to do so, and established the English lordship.

Right: The Book of Kells, 'the Arrest of Christ'. The manuscript is one of the supreme examples of Irish art, drawing on the work and development of earlier monastic art. The use of colour and designs around the strong image of man are some of the qualities which make this work unique.

Celtic Ireland

IN THE SECOND half of the first millennium BC, during what prehistorians call the Iron Age, the first Celtic peoples began to arrive in Ireland, though there is no surviving evidence of a large-scale invasion. The people known to the Greeks as Keltoi or Celts had dominated central and western Europe and spoke an Indo-European language which developed into P-Celtic, the language of Britain and Gaul, ancestor of Welsh and Breton, and Q-Celtic, the language of the Celtic inhabitants of Ireland, ancestor of Gaelic.

Celtic culture of this period is called La Tène after a site in Switzerland, and objects in the La Tène style survive mainly from the north and west of Ireland. Best known are the Turoe Stone in County Galway, and some beautifully crafted war-trumpets, golden collars or *torcs*, and decorated bronze scabbards and horse-bits. These objects seem to have belonged to a warrior society and their prevalence in Connacht and Ulster may be significant, for the latter is the setting of the *Táin Bó Cuailnge* and other great sagas of the Irish heroic age. These tales were written considerably later and should be used with caution, but they do capture something of the society that was thought to exist in Ireland in the immediate prehistoric period, a society not unlike that portrayed by contemporary descriptions of the continental Celts.

The earliest detailed account of Ireland is that by Ptolemy, an Alexandrian Greek geographer writing after AD 100, whose information may have come from Roman or British sailors familiar with the island's east coast and its main rivers, 15 of which Ptolemy notes. Of the peoples whose territories Ptolemy records, we can probably identify Dál Riata of Antrim (who were soon to found a powerful kingdom in Argyll), Dál Fiatach of Down, and Ulaid, who were later confined to Antrim and Down, though Ptolemy has them still ruling much of the north from their cult centre at Emain Macha. Emain Macha was the setting of much of the action of the early saga literature.

As Ptolemy moves from the north-east, it becomes harder to match his territories with known dynasties, and he makes no mention of the massive Iron Age earthworks at Tara, County Meath, perhaps the most important of the early royal and ritual sites. It does seem likely, though, that the *Iverni*, whom Ptolemy places in the south-west, may be the Érainn, who dominated Munster in this period: the Greek name for Ireland, *Ierne*, probably came from them, and is itself a version of the Irish word for the island, *Ériu* (later, *Éire*).

Below: The Turoe Stone, Co. Galway, is probably of La Tène period. Its purpose is unknown though most likely to be of religious significance.

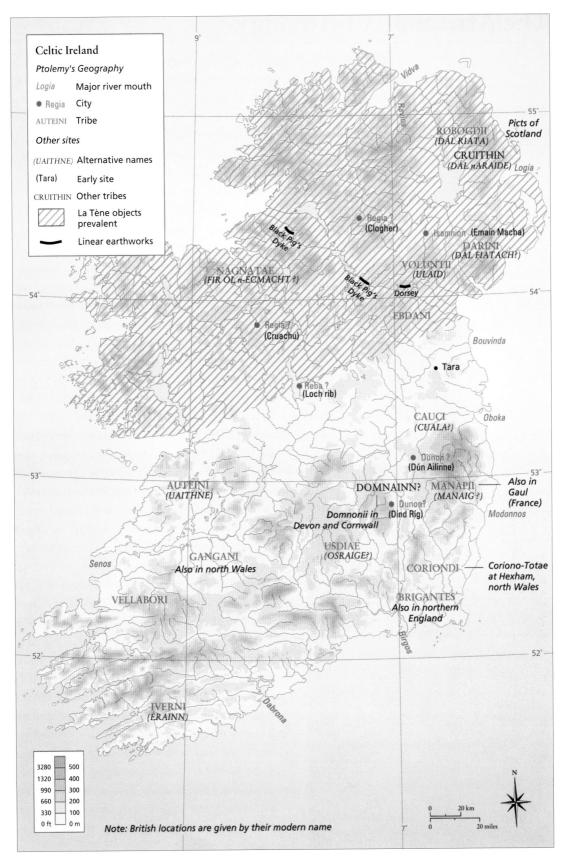

Celtic Ireland

Ptolemy's Geography

Logia — Major river mouth

● *Regia* — City

AUTEINI — Tribe

Other sites

(UAITHNE) — Alternative names

(Tara) — Early site

CRUITHIN — Other tribes

▨ — La Tène objects prevalent

▬ — Linear earthworks

Vidva

Ravios

ROBOGDII
(DÁL RIATA)

Picts of Scotland

CRUITHIN
(DÁL nARAIDE) *Logia*

55°

Black Pig's Dyke

● *Regia* ?
(Clogher)

● *Isamnion* (Emain Macha)

DARINI
(DÁL FIATACH?)

NAGNATAE
(FIR ÓL n-ECMACHT ?)

Black Pig's Dyke

VOLUNTII
(ULAID)

Dorsey

54°

EBDANI

Bouvinda

● *Regia* ?
(Cruachú)

● Tara

● *Reba* ?
(Loch rib)

CAUCI
(CUALA?)

Oboka

● *Dunon* ?
(Dún Ailinne)

53°

AUTEINI
(UAITHNE)

DOMNAINN?

MANAPII
(MANAIG ?)

Also in Gaul (France)

● *Dunon*?
(Dind Ríg)

Modonnos

Domnonii in Devon and Cornwall

USDIAE
(OSRAIGE?)

CORIONDI

Coriono-Totae at Hexham, north Wales

Senos

GANGANI
Also in north Wales

BRIGANTES
Also in northern England

VELLABORI

Birgos

52°

IVERNI
(ÉRAINN)

Dabrona

3280	500
1320	400
990	300
660	200
330	100
0 ft	0 m

N

0   20 km

0   20 miles

Note: British locations are given by their modern name

The Arrival of Christianity

ALTHOUGH Ireland lay outside the Roman Empire, it was heavily influenced by it, and evidence of trading is considerable. As Roman power in Britain weakened, by the early 5th century the Irish were not only trading and raiding there, but settling along its western coast, most successfully the Dál Riata colony in what became Scotland, but also a Déisi colony in south Wales, a Laigin (Leinster) colony in north Wales, and settlement by the Uí Liatháin in Cornwall and Devon. Such contacts with the Roman world produced the Ogham script, consisting of notches on stone based on the Latin alphabet. No doubt they also produced the first Irish encounters with Christianity.

Below: This stone from Coolmagort, Co. Kerry, displays Ogham inscriptions, the earliest written Irish.

The first Christian missionaries may have come to Ireland from Gaul in the late 4th and early 5th centuries, making it the first country outside the Roman world to be converted. The first exact date is 431, the year in which Palladius, possibly a deacon of Auxerre, was appointed by the Pope as bishop to 'the Irish who believe in Christ'. Gaulish missionaries, whose labours were probably confined largely to the east and south of Ireland, were soon superseded by British, the most famous of whom is the still highly controversial St Patrick. Patrick himself states that he was the son of an official in a city in Roman Britain, and that he was first brought to Ireland as a slave, but later returned as a bishop to preach the gospel. He was most active, it seems, north of a line from Wexford to Galway, and was particularly successful in the north-east; it was a church in this area, Armagh, because of its alleged association with Patrick, that was later to claim primacy over the rest of the Irish Church.

The cult which grew up around Patrick should not mislead us into thinking that the conversion of Ireland was quick, or largely the work of one man. We do not known anything of the activities of Palladius, but later accounts give the names of other bishops active at this period. Auxilius is said to have founded Killashee (*Cill Usailli*) near Naas, one of the royal sites associated with the kings of Leinster, while Dunshaughlin, not far from Tara, is attributed to Secundinus: in Irish it is *Domnach Sechnaill*, and sites with the element *domnach* (from Latin *dominicum*) are known to be early. Like these other early churches, Armagh is near the revered site at Emain Macha, in each case suggesting a deliberate policy of locating the new Christian churches beside old pre-Christian power-centres.

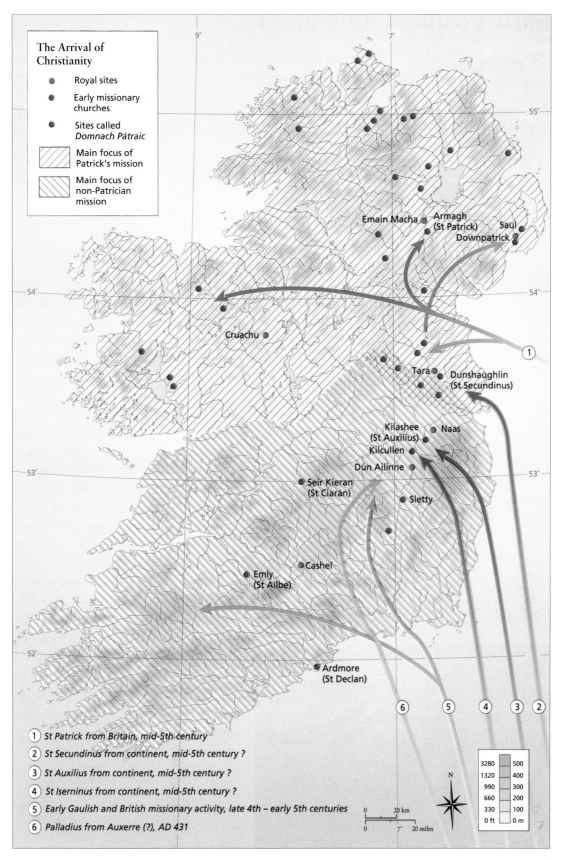

The Arrival of
Christianity

- Royal sites
- Early missionary churches
- Sites called *Domnach Pátraic*

Main focus of Patrick's mission

Main focus of non-Patrician mission

Emain Macha
Armagh (St Patrick)
Saul
Downpatrick

Cruachu

Tara
Dunshaughlin (St Secundinus)

Kilashee (St Auxilius)
Naas
Kilcullen
Dún Ailinne

Seir Kieran (St Ciarán)
Sletty

Cashel

Emly (St Ailbe)

Ardmore (St Declan)

⑥ ⑤ ④ ③ ②

① *St Patrick from Britain, mid-5th century*

② *St Secundinus from continent, mid-5th century?*

③ *St Auxilius from continent, mid-5th century?*

④ *St Iserninus from continent, mid-5th century?*

⑤ *Early Gaulish and British missionary activity, late 4th – early 5th centuries*

⑥ *Palladius from Auxerre (?), AD 431*

3280	500
1320	400
990	300
660	200
330	100
0 ft	0 m

N

0   20 km

0   20 miles

Early Peoples and Politics

Above: *Detail of a bearded warrior with spear and shield, from* The Book of Kells.

WITH THE introduction of Christianity in the 5th century came the Latin language, and with Latin came learning and literature, both in Latin and, increasingly, in the vernacular. This material, the most comprehensive to survive in any country of Dark-Age Europe, enables us to reconstruct the political map of Ireland even at this early period. The first thing that emerges is the extent to which political divisions had changed since Ptolemy's time. By the 7th century, the Érainn peoples in Munster were eclipsed by a federation of dynasties known as the Eóganachta who traced their descent from the eponymous Eógan, and who may, as their later origin-legend claimed, have been Irish colonists returned from Britain: their capital was at Cashel, which is a borrowing of the Latin castellum. To their east lay the over-kingdom of Laigin (Leinster), bounded on the west by the Barrow. Leinster originally stretched north to the Boyne, but it was pushed back to the Liffey after the 6th century, and was dominated by two dynasties, Uí Dúnlainge, centred on Kildare, and Uí Chennselaig, associated with Ferns.

The Laigin lost their lands in Meath to the Uí Néill, whose origins may lie to the west of the Shannon and who claimed descent from Niall Noígiallach ('Niall of the nine hostages'), a quasi-historical 5th-century figure. Connacht takes its name from a mythical ancestor of Niall, Conn Cétchathach ('Conn of the hundred battles'), and by the 8th century was dominated by two dynasties, Uí Briúin and Uí Fiachrach, allegedly descended from Bríon and Fiachra, brothers of Niall. By this period, Niall's reputed descendants held power in the north-west of Ireland, where they were known as the Northern Uí Néill, with a focal point at Ailech, and also in the midlands, where they are known as the Southern Uí Néill. Tara had been wrested by them from the Laigin, and the over-king of the Uí Néill bore the title 'King of Tara', which in time came to denote the high-kingship of Ireland.

Below: *Tara, perhaps the most important site in Ireland archeologically, historically and symbolically, went through many phases of occupation over many centuries, and has yet to yield up many of its secrets.*

As the Uí Néill and their subjects the Airgialla pushed north, they circumscribed the power of the Ulaid, who had earlier ruled as far south as the Boyne, defending the boundaries of their kingdom with massive linear earthworks, traces of which still survive. We do not know precisely when Emain Macha fell, but for most of the historic period the Ulaid's power was confined to the area east of the Bann, and their most important dynasty was Dál Fiatach, who ruled the Mournes from their capital at Downpatrick.

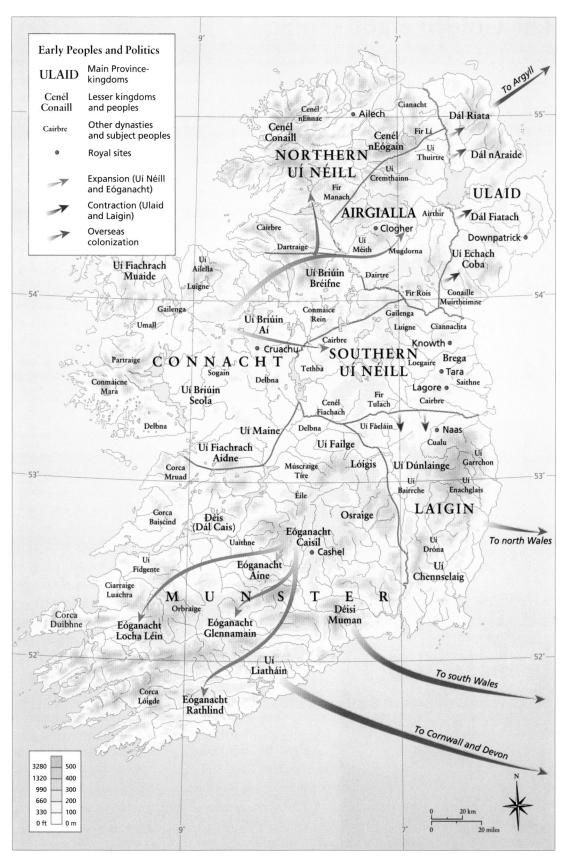

Early Peoples and Politics

ULAID — Main Province-kingdoms

Cenél Conaill — Lesser kingdoms and peoples

Cairbre — Other dynasties and subject peoples

• — Royal sites

→ — Expansion (Uí Néill and Eóganacht)

→ — Contraction (Ulaid and Laigin)

→ — Overseas colonization

To Argyll

Cenél nEnnae
• Ailech
Cianacht
Dál Riata
Cenél Conaill
Cenél nEógain
Fir Lí
Uí Thuirtre
Dál nAraide
NORTHERN UÍ NÉILL
Uí Cremthainn
ULAID
Fir Manach
AIRGIALLA
Airthir
Dál Fiatach
Cairbre
• Clogher
Uí Méith
Mugdorna
Downpatrick •
Dartraige
Dairtre
Uí Echach Coba
Uí Fiachrach Muaide
Uí Ailella
Uí Briúin Bréifne
Fir Rois
Conaille Muirtheimne
Luigne
Conmaíce Rein
Gailenga
Gailenga
Luigne
Ciannachta
Umall
Uí Briúin Aí
Cairbre
Knowth •
Partraige
• Cruachu
SOUTHERN UÍ NÉILL
Loegaire
Brega
Sogain
Tethba
Delbna
• Tara
Saithne
Conmaícne Mara
Uí Briúin Seola
Fir Tulach
Lagore •
Cairbre
Delbna
Cenél Fiachach
Delbna
Uí Fáeláin
Uí Maine
Naas
Uí Fiachrach Aidne
Uí Failge
Cualu
Corca Mruad
Múscraige Tíre
Lóigis
Uí Dúnlainge
Uí Garrchon
Éile
Uí Bairrche
Uí Enachglais
Corca Baiscind
Déis (Dál Cais)
Osraige
LAIGIN
Uaithne
Eóganacht Caisil
Uí Dróna
Uí Fidgente
Eóganacht Áine
• Cashel
Uí Chennselaig
Ciarraige Luachra
M U N S T E R
Orbraige
Corca Duibhne
Eóganacht Locha Léin
Eóganacht Glennamain
Déisi Muman
To north Wales
Uí Liatháin
To south Wales
Corca Lóigde
Eóganacht Rathlind
To Cornwall and Devon

N

3280 — 500
1320 — 400
990 — 300
660 — 200
330 — 100
0 ft — 0 m

0   20 km
0   20 miles

The Golden Age

ALTHOUGH the beginnings of a diocesan structure may have been bequeathed to the Irish Church by the early missionaries, by the 6th century Ireland's most important churches were ruled by a monastic hierarchy, many of whom were not bishops, and certain monasteries which were believed to share a common founder were grouped together in what is known as a paruchia.

The original impetus for this wave of monasticism came partly from Britain. St Enda, founder of Inis Mór, studied with St Ninian in Galloway. The Welsh saints, David and Cadoc, were the inspiration for Máedóc of Ferns and Finnian of Clonard. Finnian then taught men who became important monastic founders in their own right, including Brendan (Clonfert), Ciarán (Clonmacnoise), and Colum Cille (Durrow, Derry and Iona). The monastic centres were not the exclusive preserve of men, the most famous house of nuns being St Brigid's at Kildare, and while some churches were easily accessible and richly endowed, and undoubtedly places as much of commerce as of prayer, others, most notably Sceilg Mhicíl off the Kerry coast, were retreats from the world.

This newly Christianized and literate society soon began to display evidence of a high level of scholarship, both in Latin and Irish, clerical and secular, all of it heavily influenced by the Church. By the 7th century, Ireland's monastic schools and libraries were well-stocked with the writings of the early Church Fathers, and were beginning to produce scholars and holy men of their own, whose work was comparable with that emanating from anywhere in contemporary Christendom, and which would soon be widely disseminated throughout western Europe.

In these ecclesiastical centres, the monks themselves undoubtedly participated in manual work, but the vast extent of some monastic estates meant that the great bulk of the work was done by tenants who lived, with their families, on Church lands. This provided the monastic tenants with access to pastoral care, and the Church with a means of exploiting the economic potential of its estates. The consequence was that in this as yet pre-urban society many of the great ecclesiastical centres must have become essential hubs of economic activity.

Increasing secularization, wealth and lay-patronage enabled the monasteries to make an important contribution to the arts. Much of the finest metalwork of the period, including the famous Ardagh and Derrynaflan chalices, was produced under Church auspices, and the stone High Crosses still testify to the skill of their craftsmen, while the supreme masterpiece of ecclesiastical manuscript illumination is undoubtedly *The Book of Kells.*

Below: Muiredach's Cross at Monasterboice, Co. Louth, is among the most superb examples of the art-form. The biblical scenes carved on the east side here include Adam and Eve, the Murder of Abel, David and Goliath, Moses striking the Rock, and the Adoration of the Kings.

The Golden Age

- *Paruchia* of Patrick (churches linked to Armagh)
- *Paruchia* of Colum Cille
- Other principal monasteries and churches
- ✝ High Crosses
- Illuminated Manuscripts
- Saints trained in Britain
- Missionaries abroad

St Enda from Whithorn, early 6th century

St Colum Cille to Iona 563

St Aidan to Iona and Northumbria, 635

St Fursa to East Anglia, 633

St Finnian, from Llancarfan, c. 500

St Máedóc, from St Davids, c. 600

St Columbanus to Gaul, 591

Irish missionaries active in Britain and continent from mid-6th century

Irish scholars prevalent on the continent from early 9th century

Tory
Fahan
Derry
Raphoe
Rathlin
Coleraine
Armoy
Camus
Bodoney
Ardstraw
ULAID
Connor
Antrim
Bangor
Moville
Nendrum
Dromore
Saul
Downpatrick
NORTHERN
UÍ NÉILL
Ardboe ✝
Donaghmore ✝✝
Tynan ✝✝
Clogher
Armagh
Killevy
Inishmurray
Devenish
Boho ✝
Drumcliff
AIRGIALLA
Clones ✝
Killala
Achonry
Fenagh
Donaghmoyne
Dromiskin ✝
Louth
Linns
Monasterboice ✝✝
Termonfeckin ✝
Kilmore
Granard
Elphin
Kells (Iona?) ✝
Fore
Slane ✝
Achagower
Mayo
Baslick
Ardagh
Ardbraccan
Duleek ✝
CONNACHT
Roscommon
Inchcleraun
SOUTHERN
UÍ NÉILL
Trim
Holmpatrick
Inishbofin
Cong
Tuam
Clonard
Dunshaughlin
Finglas
Swords
Glasnevin
Annaghdown
Clonmacnoise
Durrow
Clondalkin
Tallaght
Roscam
Tihilly ✝
Killashee
Clonfert
Kinnitty ✝
Kildare
Inís Mór
Seir Kieran
Kilcullen ✝
Glendalough
Kilmacduagh
Lorrha ✝✝
Birr
Moone ✝
Kilfenora
Terryglass
Castledermot ✝
Inishcaltra
Roscrea
Killeshin
Sletty
Killaloe
Leighlin
LAIGIN
Aghade
Inis Cathaig
Mungret
Derrynaflan
Graigue-namanagh ✝
Ferns
Cashel
Kilree
Kilkeeran
Killamery ✝
St Mullins
Emly
Ahenny ✝
Begerin
Ardfert
Ardfinnan
Taghmon
MUNSTER
Lismore
Ardmore
Cork
Cloyne
Inisfallen
Sceilg Mhicíl
Ross Carbery

ft	m
3280	500
1320	400
990	300
660	200
330	100
0 ft	0 m

0   20 km
0   20 miles

N

Ireland and Europe

Above: *A carpet-page from the Evangeliary 51, an abundantly decorated book from the library of the monastery founded by St Gall, companion of St Columbanus. This volume, like others, was probably brought from Ireland, but the library also includes manuscripts written by Irish monks at St Gall.*

HAVING EARLIER witnessed the evangelizing efforts of men from Britain and mainland Europe, by the mid-6th century Ireland began to repay the debt. Although a hermit's desire to renounce home and family brought Colum Cille (Columba) to the remote Hebridean island of Iona in 563, his efforts were soon channelled into the conversion of the Picts, and his monastery, far from providing a retreat from the world, in time became the ecclesiastical capital of the Scottish kingdom of Dál Riata.

Iona monks preached the faith throughout Scotland and they later led in spreading Christianity into the Anglo-Saxon kingdom of Northumbria, their most charismatic figure being St Aidan, the first bishop of Lindisfarne, whose activities were immortalized by Bede. Other Irish *peregrini pro Christo* ('pilgrims for Christ'), like St Fursa, went further south to preach in East Anglia, having been granted as a monastic site the fortress of Cnobesburh (Burgh Castle, Suffolk). Fursa later turned his attentions towards France, where he and his brothers again became church-builders, and he was buried in the town of Péronne in Picardy which, because of its long association with Irish clerics and pilgrims, became known as *Peronna Scottorum* ('Péronne of the Irish').

In time the trickle of Irish missionary activity on the Continent became a flood, the lead being taken by Columbanus of Bangor. He and twelve disciples are said to have left Ireland for France in 591, founding the monastery of Annegray in a disused Roman fort. Having attracted numerous followers to his austere Rule, Columbanus built a new monastery at Luxeuil nearby, which became a training ground for later monastic founders. Forced out of France, Columbanus sailed up the Rhine to Lake Constance, ending up in Lombardy, where he died in his monastery of Bobbio in 615. He ranks alongside St Benedict as the 'founder of western monasticism'.

Though Irish missionaries continued to found monasteries on the Continent into the 12th century (known as *Schottenklöster*), by the 9th century they were being followed to Europe by scholars, whose learning won them positions as masters in the imperial schools of Charlemagne and his successors. The Irishman Dicuil wrote tracts on geography, grammar and astronomy. Slightly later, at Liège, Sedulius Scottus was the leading scholar-courtier, whose works of grammar, philosophy and theology are complemented by over 80 extant Latin poems. Meanwhile, at Laon, in the palace of Charles the Bald, another group of Irish scholars gathered around Ireland's brightest star in terms of European scholasticism, Johannes Scottus Eriugena.

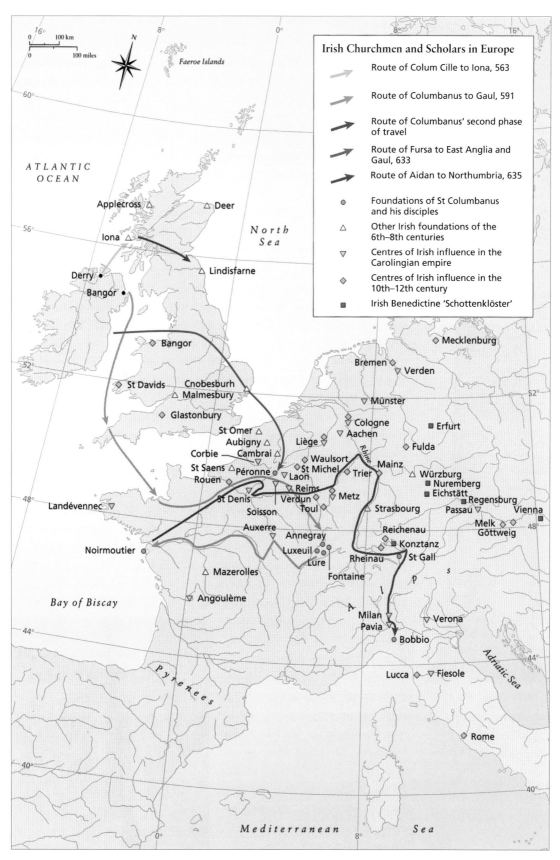

Irish Churchmen and Scholars in Europe

→ Route of Colum Cille to Iona, 563

→ Route of Columbanus to Gaul, 591

→ Route of Columbanus' second phase of travel

→ Route of Fursa to East Anglia and Gaul, 633

→ Route of Aidan to Northumbria, 635

● Foundations of St Columbanus and his disciples

△ Other Irish foundations of the 6th–8th centuries

▽ Centres of Irish influence in the Carolingian empire

◇ Centres of Irish influence in the 10th–12th century

■ Irish Benedictine 'Schottenklöster'

The Viking Wars

WHATEVER THE underlying causes, bands of Scandinavian warriors, manning fleets of technically advanced warships, began raiding western Europe in the dying years of the 8th century. The first recorded Viking attack on Ireland took place in 795 when Norse raiders assaulted several island monasteries off Ireland's coast. Raids at first tended to be confined to the northern and western seaboards, though by 824 even Sceilg in the far south-west fell victim.

In these first four decades of their campaigns, the Vikings rarely penetrated further than 20 miles inland and were still merely sea-borne raiders based elsewhere. Periodically they plundered Irish churches, not simply because Christian targets made suitable pagan prey, but because the monasteries were important focal points of economic activity, storehouses of moveable goods which were inhabited by potential captives. During the next 20 years the raids intensified and the Vikings began attacking further inland. Throughout the winter of 840–841 they stayed moored on Lough Neagh and then set up a permanent *long-phort* ('ship-camp') at Dublin, which in time became their chief settlement in Ireland, a secure base from which to launch extensive plunderings into the surrounding territories.

With permanent bases in Ireland, the Vikings themselves became vulnerable to attack, and from the mid-9th century, although they still threatened to overwhelm the country, one finds Irish kings successfully defeating them in battle. In the second half of the century the Vikings not only attacked Irish targets, but even took part in Irish warfare, allying with one Irish king in opposition to another. Danes competed with Norsemen for power over the Irish enclaves.

By the mid-850s great raids were on the decline, and the Vikings turned their attention further afield, to northern Britain and Iceland. Divisions within the Norse communities in Ireland, and more effective Irish opposition, led to their expulsion from Dublin in 902, and no further Irish Viking activity is recorded until 914, when Viking fleets reappeared in Waterford harbour, attacked Munster and Leinster, re-occupied Dublin and scored some notable victories against the Irish kings. For the next two decades the Dublin Vikings were very powerful and sought to reign over the kingdom of York and over the Norse of Waterford and Limerick. Thereafter their power declined, and the activities of the Dublin Norse were generally confined to the town's hinterland. By about 950 this last great phase of Viking warfare was at an end.

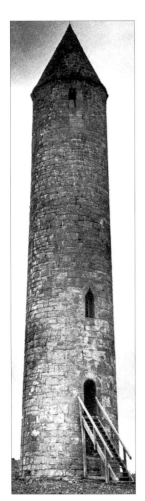

Above: Round towers, though primarily bell-towers, perhaps served as lookouts and refuges. This fine example at Devenish shows the entrance well above ground and easy to defend.

Right: Unearthed in Dublin, this drawing on a ship plank shows a man high in the rigging of a Viking ship.

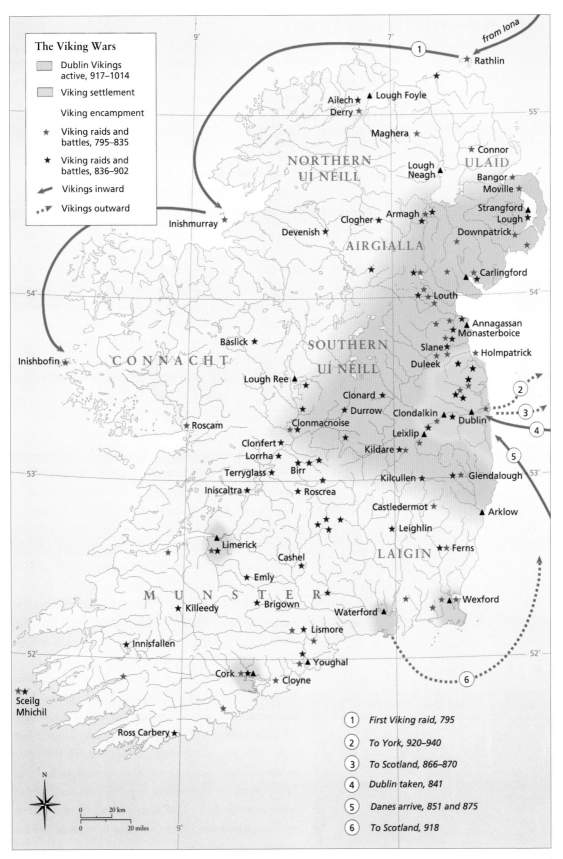

from Iona

The Viking Wars

Dublin Vikings active, 917–1014

Viking settlement

Viking encampment

★ Viking raids and battles, 795–835

★ Viking raids and battles, 836–902

← Vikings inward

▸ Vikings outward

① First Viking raid, 795

② To York, 920–940

③ To Scotland, 866–870

④ Dublin taken, 841

⑤ Danes arrive, 851 and 875

⑥ To Scotland, 918

Rathlin

Ailech ★   ▲ Lough Foyle
Derry ★

Maghera ★

★ Connor

NORTHERN
UÍ NÉILL

Lough Neagh ▲

ULAID

Bangor ★
Moville ★

Strangford ★
Lough ★

Clogher ★   Armagh ★★★

Downpatrick ★

Devenish ★

AIRGIALLA

Inishmurray ★

★★ ★

★ Carlingford ▲

★★ Louth

Baslick ★

SOUTHERN
UÍ NÉILL

★ ▲ Annagassan
Monasterboice ▲

Inishbofin ★

CONNACHT

Slane ★★

★ Holmpatrick

Duleek ★

Lough Ree ▲

Clonard ★

★ Durrow

Clondalkin ★ ▲
Leixlip ★ ▲   Dublin ▲

★ Roscam

Clonmacnoise ★★

Kildare ★★

Clonfert ★
Lorrha ★

Terryglass ★   Birr ★★★

Kilcullen ★   ★★ Glendalough

Iniscaltra ★   ★ Roscrea

Castledermot ★

▲ Arklow

★★ Limerick ▲

Cashel ★

Leighlin ★

LAIGIN

★★ Ferns

★ Emly

Killeedy ★   ★ Brigown

★ ▲ Wexford

Waterford ▲

★★ Lismore

★ Innisfallen

★ ▲ Youghal

Cork ★★▲   ★ Cloyne

★★
Sceilg
Mhichil

Ross Carbery ★

N

0   20 km
0   20 miles

25

The Age of Brian Boru

IT WOULD BE wrong to exaggerate the ill-effects of Viking attacks on the Irish Church, since the latter was already highly politicized, and monastic centres sometimes suffered as much from the depredations of rival Irish rulers as from Viking assaults. The Ostmen, as they called themselves, made many positive contributions to Irish life. They gave the country its first towns, its first coinage and more advanced naval technology. As some of their settlements grew into towns, they expanded Ireland's trading contacts and introduced its artists and craftsmen to new styles and motifs. Dublin became one of the wealthiest ports in western Europe.

The Ostmen generally governed large areas of their towns' hinterland, and in so doing displaced some minor local kingdoms. Their strength in Munster may have contributed to the decline of the reigning Eóganachta kings and to the ascendancy of the rulers of Dál Cais, who controlled the strategic lower Shannon basin. The first of their kings to attain real power was Cennétig mac Lorcáin who died as king of Thomond (north Munster) in 951, to be succeeded by his son, Mathgamain, who brought east Munster, and the Ostmen of Limerick and Waterford, under his sway. After Mathgamain's death in 976, his brother Brian Boru succeeded. He is usually regarded as the greatest of Ireland's high-kings.

Below: Brian Boru, high-king of Ireland. This fanciful image, made many hundreds of years after his death, indicates a fond folk memory of this king who is popularly thought to have banished the Vikings from Ireland.

Brian quickly rose to power, overshadowing his Eóganachta rivals to make himself king of all Munster. At this point he emerged as a challenge to the reign-

ing high-king of Ireland, Máel Sechnaill mac Domnaill of the Southern Uí Néill, who in 997 acknowledged Brian as king over the southern half of Ireland (*Leth Moga*) and who finally submitted to Brian as high-king in 1002. In 1005, Brian set about asserting his dominance throughout the island, using the title 'Emperor of the Irish'. A revolt by the Leinstermen and the Ostmen of Dublin, who also raised Viking aid from Man and the Western Isles, led to Brian's great victory over them in the battle of Clontarf in 1014, at which, however, Brian himself was slain.

Brian's achievement was considerable. Early medieval Ireland did not possess a monarch whose rule was effective over the entire island, but the Uí Néill, who dominated the northern half of the island (*Leth Cuinn*), were often able to compel most, if not all, of the other province-kings to submit to them as high-king. Brian Boru, however, by making himself high-king of all Ireland, ended the Uí Néill monopoly of the title. Others in subsequent generations attempted to emulate him but none was as successful.

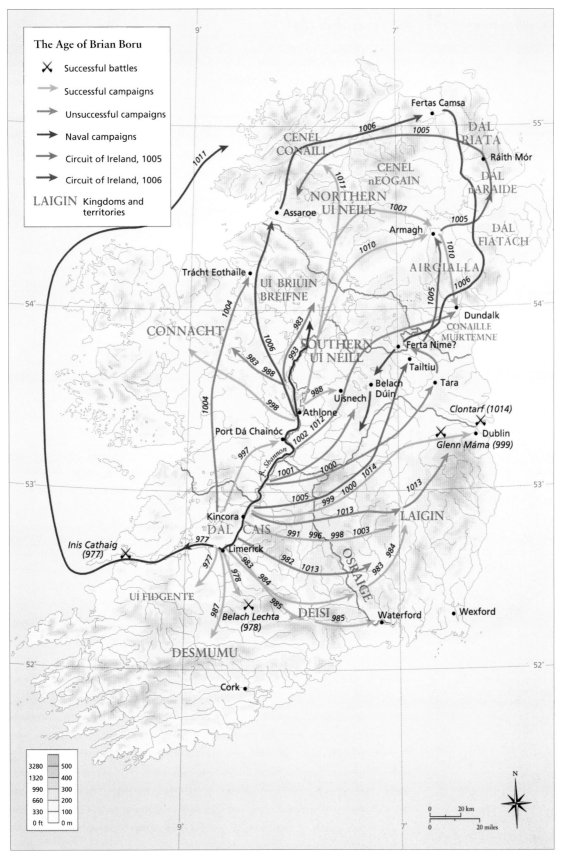

The Age of Brian Boru

✗ Successful battles

→ Successful campaigns

→ Unsuccessful campaigns

→ Naval campaigns

→ Circuit of Ireland, 1005

→ Circuit of Ireland, 1006

LAIGIN Kingdoms and territories

Fertas Camsa

DÁL RIATA

Ráith Mór

DÁL nARAIDE

CENÉL CONAILL

CENÉL nEOGAIN

NORTHERN UÍ NÉILL

Assaroe

Armagh

DÁL FIATACH

AIRGIALLA

Trácht Eothaile

UÍ BRIÚIN BRÉIFNE

Dundalk

CONAILLE MUIRTEMNE

CONNACHT

SOUTHERN UÍ NÉILL

Ferta Nime?

Tailtiu

Tara

Belach Dúin

Uisnech

Athlone

Clontarf (1014)

Dublin

Glenn Máma (999)

Port Dá Chaínóc

R. Shannon

LAIGIN

Kincora

DÁL CAIS

OSRAIGE

Inis Cathaig (977)

Limerick

Wexford

UÍ FIDGENTE

Belach Lechta (978)

DÉISI

Waterford

DESMUMU

Cork

3280 — 500
1320 — 400
990 — 300
660 — 200
330 — 100
0 ft — 0 m

N

0   20 km
0   20 miles

Reform of the Church

FROM THE mid-11th century the Church throughout western Christendom underwent a reformation generally known as the Gregorian movement. The abuses afflicting the Church elsewhere were not absent from the Irish Church, which by then had a largely married and hereditary clergy, with individuals not in holy orders holding high office. Abbots exercised more power than bishops, and there was an absence of territorially-based dioceses and parishes. The morals of the laity were also thought in need of reform since Irish (Brehon) law allowed divorce and tolerated marriage within the Church's forbidden degrees of consanguinity.

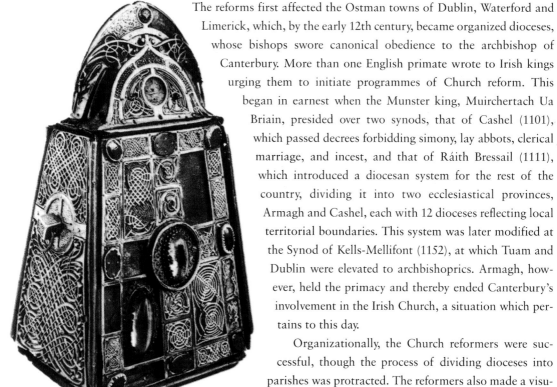

Above: *A reliquary, the shrine of St Patrick's bell, made around the beginning of the 12th century to house an iron bell, traditionally believed to have belonged to the Saint.*

The reforms first affected the Ostman towns of Dublin, Waterford and Limerick, which, by the early 12th century, became organized dioceses, whose bishops swore canonical obedience to the archbishop of Canterbury. More than one English primate wrote to Irish kings urging them to initiate programmes of Church reform. This began in earnest when the Munster king, Muirchertach Ua Briain, presided over two synods, that of Cashel (1101), which passed decrees forbidding simony, lay abbots, clerical marriage, and incest, and that of Ráith Bressail (1111), which introduced a diocesan system for the rest of the country, dividing it into two ecclesiastical provinces, Armagh and Cashel, each with 12 dioceses reflecting local territorial boundaries. This system was later modified at the Synod of Kells-Mellifont (1152), at which Tuam and Dublin were elevated to archbishoprics. Armagh, however, held the primacy and thereby ended Canterbury's involvement in the Irish Church, a situation which pertains to this day.

Organizationally, the Church reformers were successful, though the process of dividing dioceses into parishes was protracted. The reformers also made a visual impact: Cormac's Chapel at Cashel, for example, is a notable example of the new style of Irish Romanesque architecture, and was commissioned by the king of South Munster (Desmond), Cormac MacCarthaig. Where the reforms failed were in their attempts to eradicate abuses in both the Church and society. Despite these failures, the Irish Church produced its fair share of saintly bishops, the most illustrious of whom was St Malachy Ua Morgair, who helped end hereditary succession to the see of Armagh, and who was heavily involved in the reorganization of Irish monasticism. He converted older Irish monastic houses into convents of canons following the rule of St Augustine, and having visited St Bernard's abbey of Clairvaux in France, in 1142 he established a Cistercian abbey at Mellifont, County Louth. Over a dozen similar abbeys were founded in the next 20 years.

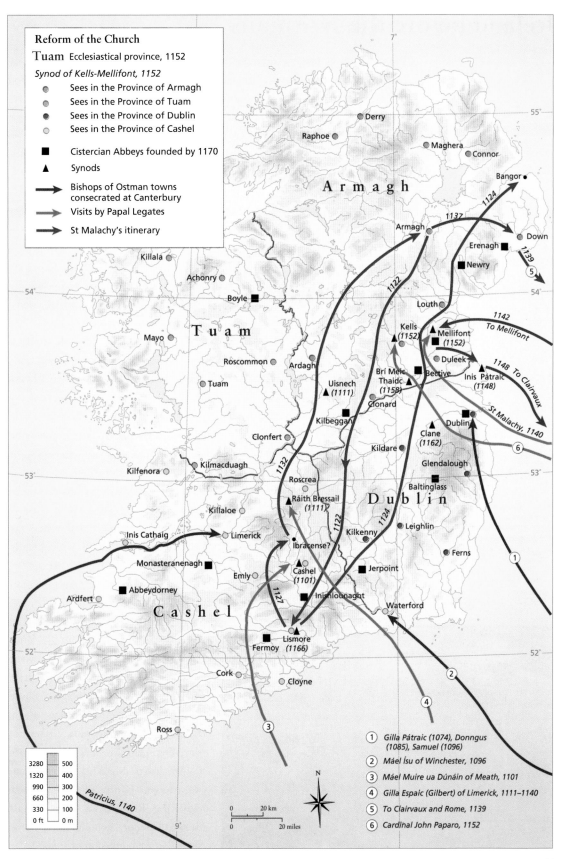

Reform of the Church

Tuam Ecclesiastical province, 1152

Synod of Kells-Mellifont, 1152

- Sees in the Province of Armagh
- Sees in the Province of Tuam
- Sees in the Province of Dublin
- Sees in the Province of Cashel

■ Cistercian Abbeys founded by 1170

▲ Synods

→ Bishops of Ostman towns consecrated at Canterbury

→ Visits by Papal Legates

→ St Malachy's itinerary

① Gilla Pátraic (1074), Donngus (1085), Samuel (1096)
② Máel Ísu of Winchester, 1096
③ Máel Muire ua Dúnáin of Meath, 1101
④ Gilla Espaic (Gilbert) of Limerick, 1111–1140
⑤ To Clairvaux and Rome, 1139
⑥ Cardinal John Paparo, 1152

Ireland before the Normans

BRIAN BORU'S lasting achievement was his demonstration that any province-king could make himself master of the whole island, provided his armies were strong enough. The Uí Néill, in the person of Máel Sechnaill mac Domnaill, retook the high-kingship after 1014, but with the latter's death in 1022, the title lay in abeyance. For 50 years no province-king emerged powerful enough to force his enemies into submission and make the title effective.

For most of the middle years of the 11th century, the leading contender for the high-kingship was the Leinster king, Diarmait MacMáil na mBó, who involved himself in the affairs of England and Wales, and whose power was greatly increased in 1052 when he assumed the kingship of Dublin, the first Irish king ever to do so. The practice was repeated by later claimants to the high-kingship, who sometimes appointed their intended heir king of Dublin, which in the process came to replace Tara as symbolic capital of the country.

During this twilight period Irish kingship underwent considerable changes. Wars lasted longer and were more frequent. Kings exercised more power, promulgating laws and imposing taxes, and employing an increasing variety of officials. Besides being the chosen leader of a people, kings became owners of the land, which they could grant by charter to the Church or to their vassals in return for military service, rather like feudal kings elsewhere. They invaded and conquered neighbouring kingdoms, dividing them among their allies or appointing puppet-rulers to govern them under their overlordship.

From 1072 until 1086, Brian Boru's grandson Tairdelbach Ua Briain claimed the high-kingship, though his son Muirchertach (1086–1119) was a more effective ruler, famous for his marriage-alliances with the king of Norway and the Normans of South Wales, and a leading patron of Church reform. Subsequently, the power of the Uí Briain (O'Briens) waned and shifted northwards. The Connacht king, Tairdelbach Ua Conchobhair (O'Connor) was probably the most effective 12th-century high-king, a prodigious builder of fortresses and bridges and master of an effective army and fleet. A declining force in his latter years, he was succeeded in 1156 by the king of the Northern Uí Néill, Muirchertach Mac Lochlainn, whose leading ally was the Leinster King, Diarmait MacMurchada (Dermot MacMurrough). Mac Lochlainn's death in 1166 led to MacMurchada's expulsion overseas by the allies of the new high-King Ruaidrí Ua Conchobhair (Rory O'Connor), and ultimately to the Anglo-Norman invasion of Ireland.

Below: Excavations at Fishamble Street and Wood Quay in Dublin revealed the wealth and significance of pre-Norman Dublin, which by the 12th century had become the capital of Ireland in everything but name. This photograph shows a good example of a fairly typical Hiberno-Scandinavian house.

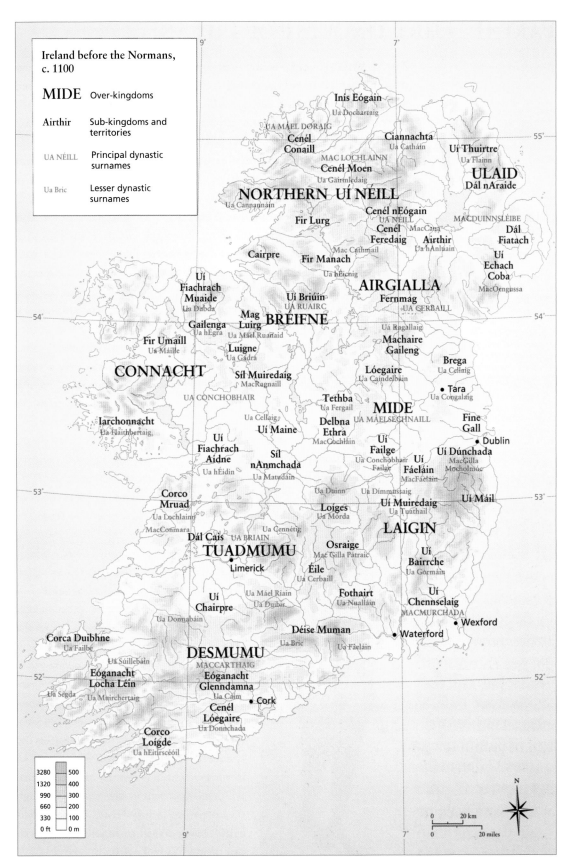

Ireland before the Normans, c. 1100

MIDE — Over-kingdoms

Airthir — Sub-kingdoms and territories

UA NÉILL — Principal dynastic surnames

Ua Bric — Lesser dynastic surnames

Inis Eógain
Ua Dochartaig

UA MÁEL DORAIG
Cenél
Conaill

Ciannachta
Ua Catháin

Uí Thuirtre
Ua Flainn

MAC LOCHLAINN
Cenél Moen
Ua Gairmledaig

ULAID
Dál nAraide

NORTHERN UÍ NÉILL

Cenél nEógain
UA NÉILL
Cenél · MacCana
Feredaig   Airthir
Mac Cáthmáil   Ua hAnluain

MACDUINNSLÉIBE
Dál
Fiatach

Fir Lurg

Cairpre   Fir Manach
Ua hEicnig

Uí
Echach
Coba
MacOengussa

Uí
Fiachrach
Muaide
Ua Dubda

Uí Briúin
UA RUAIRC

AIRGIALLA
Fernmag
UA CERBAILL

Mag
Luirg   BRÉIFNE

Uá Ragallaig

Gailenga
Ua hEgra   Ua Máel Ruanaid

Machaire
Gaileng

Fir Umaill
Ua Máille

Luigne
Ua Gádra

Brega
Ua Cellaig

CONNACHT

Síl Muiredaig
MacRagnaill

Lóegaire
Ua Caindelbáin

UA CONCHOBHAIR

Tethba
Ua Fergail

MIDE
UA MÁELSECHNAILL

Tara
Ua Congalaig

Iarchonnacht
Ua Flaithbertaig,

Ua Cellaig

Uí Maine

Delbna
Ethra
MacCochláin

Fine
Gall

Uí
Fiachrach
Aidne
Ua hÉidin

Síl
nAnmchada
Ua Matudáin

Uí
Failge
Ua Conchobhair
Failge

Uí
Fáeláin
MacFáeláin

Dublin

Uí Dúnchada
MacGilla
Mocholmóc

Corco
Mruad
Ua Lochlainn
MacConmara

Ua Duinn   Ua Dimmussaig

Uí Muiredaig
Ua Tuathail

Uí Máil

Dál Cais   UA BRIAIN
TUADMUMU
Limerick

Loiges
Ua Mórda

LAIGIN

Ua Cennétig

Osraige
Mac Gilla Pátraic

Éile
Ua Cerbaill

Uí
Bairrche
Ua Górmáin

Uí
Chairpre
Ua Donnabáin

Ua Máel Riain
Ua Duibir

Fothairt
Ua Nualláin

Uí
Chennselaig
MACMURCHADA

Wexford

Corca Duibhne
Ua Failbe

Déise Muman
Ua Bric   Ua Fáeláin

Waterford

DESMUMU
MACCARTHAIG

Ua Ségda

Eóganacht
Locha Léin
Ua Muirchertaig

Eóganacht
Glenndamna
Ua Cáim

Cork

Cenél
Lóegaire
Ua Donnchada

Corco
Loígde
Ua hEitirscéóil

3280	500
1320	400
990	300
660	200
330	100
0 ft	0 m

N

0   20 km
0   20 miles

PART II: THE CONQUEST OF IRELAND

Brendan Smith

THE ELEVENTH and twelfth centuries were a time of expansion throughout western Europe typified by a growth in population and an upturn in economic activity which resulted in a dramatic increase in the number and size of towns. Another consequence of this pressure of population was a colonial movement which saw lords and peasants from Europe's central zone settling in peripheral regions such as the Slav lands of eastern Germany and the Celtic lands of the British Isles. This was also an era of tremendous intellectual advance as ancient disciplines such as law, philosophy and theology came under vigorous re-examination, a process which gave rise to the earliest universities in western Europe at Paris and Bologna. Religious reform was also in the air as the Church sought to meet popular demands for higher standards among the clergy and began to emphasize a more personal approach to spirituality which stressed the individual's relationship to God. New religious orders such as the Augustinians and Cistercians offered a communal existence distant from the world, while the papacy embarked on a campaign to strengthen its authority within society as a whole. With the launching of the First Crusade, aimed at liberating Jerusalem, in 1095 by Pope Urban II, western Europe declared to the wider world a new-found energy and sense of purpose.

Below: This illustration features Diarmait MacMurchada from a manuscript of Topographia Hiberniae *by Giraldus Cambrensis, copied c. 1200. Diarmait was instrumental in initiating the English invasion and has a reputation as a ruthless warlord. Hence his depiction bearing the archetypal long axe borrowed by the Irish from the Vikings.*

Intimately involved in all these developments were the Normans, a people descended from Viking raiders who had settled in north-west France in the 9th century. By 1100 the Normans controlled both southern Italy and England and were helping to establish the new Crusader states in Palestine. In the short term their success rested on their martial prowess, but in the long term it was their adaptability and readiness to integrate with the peoples they conquered which secured their achievements. In England, for instance, in the years after the victory at Hastings in 1066 they formed a small ruling élite, fearful of the conquered population which surrounded them, but within a century they ceased to see themselves as foreigners and, although they remained largely French in speech and culture, were happy to be called — and to call themselves — English.

Below: *Carrickfergus castle, Co. Antrim, built by John de Courcy, was among the first stone castles to dominate the local population.*

Kings of England since 1066 had expressed occasional interest in dominating Ireland, and it was no surprise that the English should have become involved there in the 12th century. It was far from inevitable, however, that such involvement would take the form it did, that of conquest. In Scotland, Normans from England were introduced in the early 12th century under the controlling hand of the Scots king himself, and a successful blending of old and new aristocratic elements allowed Scotland to retain its position as an independent kingdom for the rest of the Middle Ages.

In Ireland, however, the existence of competing dynasties such as the Uí Néill, Uí Chonchobhair and MacMurchada on the one hand, and the failure to establish a system of succession to kingship which prevented internecine strife on the other, meant that once the English arrived in the country they were able to play different factions off against each other and to secure their own independence from the native kings.

The attitude of King Henry II was crucial in determining the character of English intervention in Ireland. He might have been reluctant to become involved, but once Strongbow had proved successful, Henry took control of the operation, thereby ensuring both that Ireland would pose no threat to England and that its rich lands would be his alone to bestow upon his favourites. Although only two kings, John and Richard II, visited Ireland in the rest of the Middle Ages, the precedent of direct royal control over Irish affairs had been set.

It soon became clear that not all the native ruling families in Ireland could be displaced and that English settlers would not come in sufficient numbers to turn the island into a 'little England'. Even the most independent Irish kings recognized the English King as their overlord, but at a local level they acknowledged the authority of a neighbouring English lord only if he was strong enough to enforce their compliance. The English did not extend to the Irish their own laws, an omission which worked to the disadvantage of the native population and served to heighten ill-feeling between the two peoples. Many of the settlers assimilated culturally with their Irish neighbours over time, but this provoked harsh condemnation from the more conservative elements in colonial society, who passed

Below: *This effigy of Thomas de Cantwell in Kilfane Church, Co. Kilkenny, shows a stylized image of an Anglo-Norman knight.*

legislation, such as the Statutes of Kilkenny of 1366, to prevent the English from adopting Irish ways. Over time the settler community began to identify increasingly with Ireland and to resent the men from England who were commissioned to rule them, and the policies of the 15th century were dominated by the great settler families of Butler and FitzGerald.

The equilibrium between the two nations in Ireland could not withstand the reinvigoration of English government under Henry VII and Henry VIII, and the destruction of the ruling magnates propelled Ireland into the disastrous chaos of the 16th century.

Below: Richard II, the last English King to visit Ireland before 1689, made two expeditions to the country, in 1394-5 and 1399. The illustration shows a meeting between Richard's representative the Earl of Gloucester, and Diarmait MacMurchada's descendant, the reigning King of Leinster, Art MacMurchada Caomhánach. The English cavalry are depicted heavily armoured, the redoubtable Art considerably less so and riding without stirrups in the usual Irish fashion.

35

The English Invasion

DIARMAIT MacMurchada's expulsion from Ireland in 1166 set in train a series of events which within ten years saw the kings of Ireland accept the king of England as their lord and saw vast parts of the island fall into the hands of English barons.

MacMurchada travelled first to Bristol, with whose merchants he already had contacts, and from there made his way to France to find Henry II. After acknowledging Henry as his lord, Diarmait was given permission to recruit fighting men in England to help him recover his position in Ireland. It was among the marcher lords of south Wales that he found his first recruits.

A century of conflict with the Welsh had made these men particularly receptive to his promises of new lands waiting to be won by the sword, and their enthusiasm was sharpened by the knowledge that they did not enjoy the favour of their king. Their leader, Richard FitzGilbert, better known as Strongbow, had supported Henry's opponent, King Stephen, in the civil war which troubled England in the 1130s and 1140s, and he and his followers received no patronage from Henry after he become king in 1154.

MacMurchada returned to Ireland in 1167 and quickly re-established his position with the help of a small body of foreign knights. Strongbow arrived with a larger force in August 1170 and, with much bloodshed, he and Diarmait together took the Ostman city of Waterford. At this point Strongbow received his reward from Diarmait by marrying MacMurchada's daughter, Aoife. Dublin was taken a few weeks later, the province of Meath was invaded, and English forces raided the kingdom of Bréifne. Diarmait's death in May 1171, without legitimate male heirs, meant that his kingdom of Leinster came into Strongbow's possession through Aoife.

Below: The seal of Richard FitzGilbert de Clare, lord of Pembroke, alias Strongbow, the Norman marcher lord and leader of a group of Norman warrior lords based in the Welsh border lands.

This was the signal for Henry II to intervene. He was already suspicious of Strongbow. Although he had given Strongbow permission to go to Ireland, Henry was determined to stop an independent kingdom emerging under his rule. The king landed at Waterford with a large force in October 1171 and received acknowledgement of his position as lord of Ireland from both the new conquerors and several of the native kings, though probably not the high-king, Ruaidrí Ua Conchobhair (Rory O'Connor). Strongbow had already offered his subjugation to the King and, having made his royal progress from his landing place to the city of Dublin, Henry II formally granted Leinster to Strongbow in return for homage and performance of military service.

At a stroke Ireland had been added to the lands of the king of England, lands which stretched from the Scottish border to the Pyrenees. Ireland had been brought into the European mainstream, but on terms which were not its own.

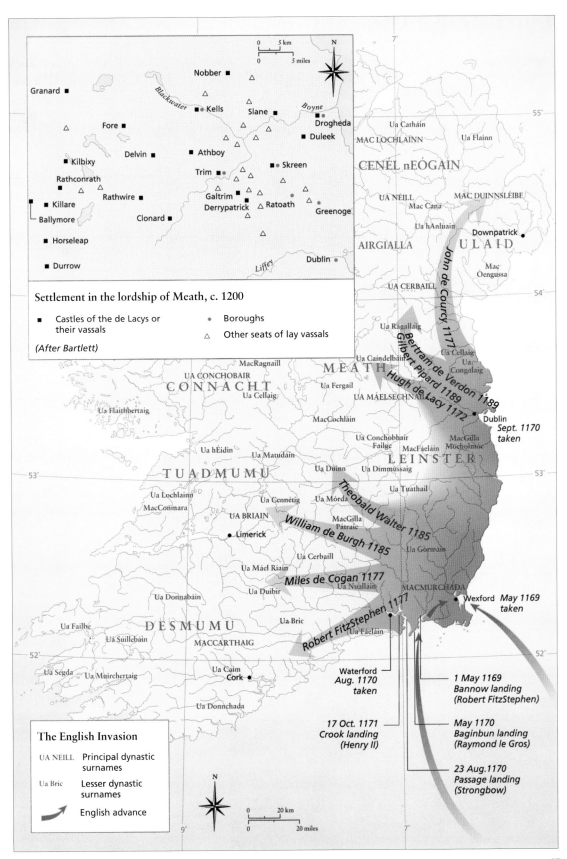

Settlement in the lordship of Meath, c. 1200

■ Castles of the de Lacys or their vassals

● Boroughs

△ Other seats of lay vassals

(After Bartlett)

The English Invasion

UA NEILL Principal dynastic surnames

Ua Bric Lesser dynastic surnames

➤ English advance

Dublin *Sept. 1170 taken*

Wexford *May 1169 taken*

Waterford *Aug. 1170 taken*

1 May 1169 *Bannow landing (Robert FitzStephen)*

17 Oct. 1171 *Crook landing (Henry II)*

May 1170 *Baginbun landing (Raymond le Gros)*

23 Aug. 1170 *Passage landing (Strongbow)*

John de Courcy 1177
Bertram de Verdon 1189
Gilbert Pipard 1189
Hugh de Lacy 1172
Theobald Walter 1185
William de Burgh 1185
Miles de Cogan 1177
Robert FitzStephen 1177

MAC LOCHLAINN
CENÉL nEÓGAIN
UA NÉILL
Mac Cana
AIRGIALLA
UA CERBAILL
Ua Cathái n
Ua Flainn
MAC DUINNSLÉIBE
Ua hAnluain
ULAID
Downpatrick
Mac Óengussa

Ua Ragallaig
Ua Cellaig
Ua Congalaig
Ua Caindelbáin
MEATH
Ua Fergail
UA MÁELSECHNAILL
MacCochláin
Ua Conchobhair Failge
MacGilla Mocholmóc
MacFáeláin
LEINSTER
Dublin

MacRagnaill
UA CONCHOBAIR
CONNACHT
Ua Cellaig
Ua Flaithbertaig

Ua hÉidin
Ua Matudáin
Ua Duinn
Ua Dimmussaig
Ua Tuathail

TUADMUMU
Ua Lochlainn
MacConmara
UA BRIAIN
Limerick
Ua Cennétig
Ua Mórda
MacGilla Pátraic
Ua Gormain
Ua Cerbaill

Ua Máel Riain
Ua Duibir
Ua Nuallain
MACMURCHADA

Ua Donnabáin
Ua Bric
Ua Fáeláin

Ua Failbe
DESMUMU
Ua Suillebáin
MACCARTHAIG

Ua Ségda Ua Muirchertaig
Cork
Ua Caim

Ua Donnchada

Inset map (Settlement in the lordship of Meath):
Granard
Nobber
Blackwater
Kells
Slane
Boyne
Drogheda
Duleek
Fore
Delvin
Athboy
Skreen
Kilbixy
Rathconrath
Trim
Galtrim
Derrypatrick
Ratoath
Greenoge
Killare
Rathwire
Ballymore
Clonard
Horseleap
Durrow
Liffey
Dublin

0 5 km
0 5 miles

0 20 km
0 20 miles

37

Expansion of the Colony

Above: *A carving representing an Anglo-Irish noblewoman, believed to be the first Countess of Ormond, in St Mary's Church at Gowran, near Kilkenny.*

THE CONQUERORS found it relatively easy at first to defeat the Irish in battle. What made their involvement in Irish history so crucial, however, was not their military success, but rather what they chose to do with the lands they had won. It was colonization rather than conquest which changed the course of Irish history after 1171.

Upon entering enemy territory the invaders would first construct a large mound of raised earth with a flat top surrounded by a fence, and would then build a wooden tower on its summit. This primitive castle, known as a 'motte', could be defended with ease and provided a base from which cattle raids could be launched into the lands of the local Irish king. When the local king had been subdued, the leader of the invading force would divide the best land in the territory among his supporters, a process known as subinfeudation.

At this point the emphasis changed from military conquest to economic exploitation. The conquerors had made a long-term investment in Ireland and expected wealth in return. To achieve this they imported the agricultural system, based on the manor and on a mixture of arable and pastoral farming techniques, with which they were familiar in England. Irish peasants were not removed from the land but there was a need for more labourers and so the recruitment of English peasants and artisans began. Land was scarce in England at the time and the promise of new farmland and improved conditions of tenure attracted many settlers. The ports of Bristol and Chester served as points of departure for migrants who, for the most part, came from the west midlands and south-west of England. The legacy of this movement of people is seen in Ireland today in common surnames such as Bermingham, Stafford, Dowdall (Dovedale, Derbyshire) and Bruton (Somerset).

As a result of this colonial movement the landscape of much of Ireland was dramatically transformed in the space of a few generations. New towns such as Drogheda, Dundalk, Carrickfergus, Sligo, Athenry, Nenagh, New Ross, Kilkenny and Trim sprang up, their city walls and impressive castles a reminder that this was a land of conquest. In the countryside woods were cleared, arable cultivation expanded and the volume of internal and foreign trade soared. In all its history Ireland has never experienced an economic boom quite like that of the 13th century.

Left: *In many parts of Ireland the English raised mottes to defend their newly acquired territories. They were often constructed in or near an existing population site in order to exploit the maximum economic potential. This motte is at Clonard, close to the early Christian monastic settlement.*

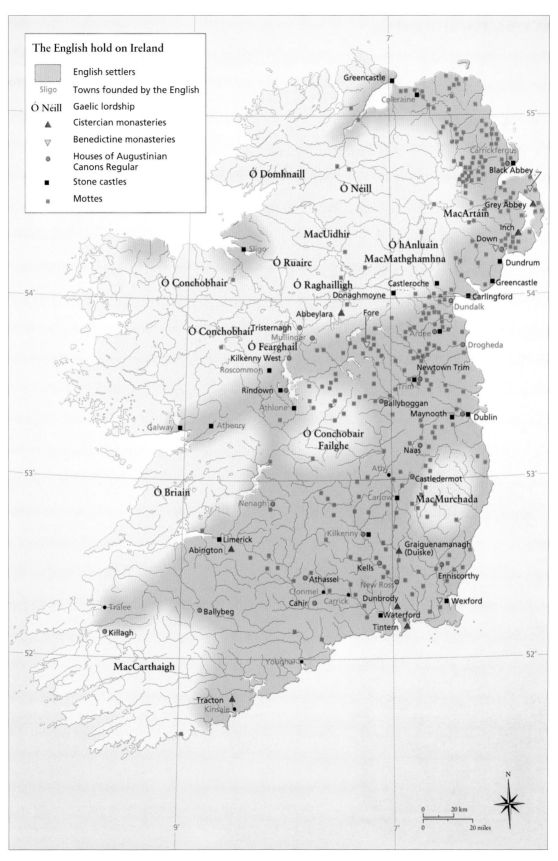

The English hold on Ireland

- English settlers
- *Sligo* — Towns founded by the English
- Ó Néill — Gaelic lordship
- ▲ Cistercian monasteries
- ▽ Benedictine monasteries
- ● Houses of Augustinian Canons Regular
- ■ Stone castles
- ▪ Mottes

Greencastle
Coleraine
Carrickfergus
Black Abbey
Ó Domhnaill
Ó Néill
Grey Abbey
MacArtáin
Inch
Down
MacUidhir
Ó hAnluain
Dundrum
Ó Ruairc
MacMathghamhna
Ó Conchobhair
Ó Raghaill1igh
Castleroche
Greencastle
Donaghmoyne
Carlingford
Dundalk
Abbeylara
Fore
Ó Conchobhair
Tristernagh
Drogheda
Mullingar
Ardee
Ó Fearghail
Kilkenny West
Newtown Trim
Roscommon
Rindown
Trim
Athlone
Ballyboggan
Maynooth
Galway
Athenry
Dublin
Ó Conchobair
Failghe
Naas
Ó Briain
Athy
Castledermot
Nenagh
Carlow
MacMurchada
Limerick
Kilkenny
Graiguenamanagh
Abington
(Duiske)
Kells
Enniscorthy
Athassel
New Ross
Clonmel
Dunbrody
Wexford
Cahir
Carrick
Tralee
Ballybeg
Waterford
Tintern
Killagh
Youghal
MacCarthaigh
Tracton
Kinsale

N

0   20 km
0   20 miles

Irish Resistance

RORY O'CONNOR was sufficiently powerful to force most of the important Irish kings to join him in an attack on Dublin after its capture by Strongbow, but he proved an inept military commander and his army was scattered with heavy losses. Upon the arrival of Henry II many native kings rushed to submit to him, following the advice of their bishops who saw Henry as the man to bring the Irish Church into line with the rest of Europe.

Armed resistance to the invaders did not, of course, cease completely, but the brutal treatment of those who did continue to oppose the new regime served as a powerful disincentive to others contemplating raiding the new towns and settlements or planning other forms of rebellion. Tigernán O'Rourke, king of Breifne, was treacherously slain on his way to a parley in 1172, and his head and decapitated corpse displayed at various points on the walls of Dublin after the deed.

For those kings who survived the initial English onslaught, the path of survival lay in accommodation with the new regime and in the consolidation of local power.

Below: *A galloglass* (gall-óglach, *'foreign warrior'), imported from the west of Scotland. These heavily armoured and well-equipped fighters affected the balance of power.*

The way of compromise, however, was not to last. Piecemeal English advance continued throughout the 13th century, and even the most compliant kings such as Feidlim O'Connor — who fought for the English in Wales in 1245 — found they could not trust the king of England to keep his promises. By the 1250s a reaction had set in and, in 1258, the most important native rulers challenged the English by recognizing Brian O'Neill as high-king of Ireland. Two years later O'Neill's forces were defeated by the colonists at the battle of Down, and his severed head was sent to England for public display at the Tower of London.

With O'Neill died the last attempt to revive the high-kingship of Ireland for a native claimant, but the whole episode was not without future significance. In 1259 Aed O'Connor, son of the king of Connacht, who was with Brian at Down, had married a princess from the west of Scotland who brought back with her to Ireland a force of 160 'galloglass', the fierce mercenary soldiers from the Hebrides. The subsequent employment of galloglass by other Irish kings reduced the military advantage which the English had previously enjoyed.

Irish resistance in the century after the English arrived was, generally speaking, sporadic, uncoordinated and prompted by local rather than national concerns, but it did ensure the survival of the most important native dynasties and guaranteed that the English settlers could never rest easy in Ireland.

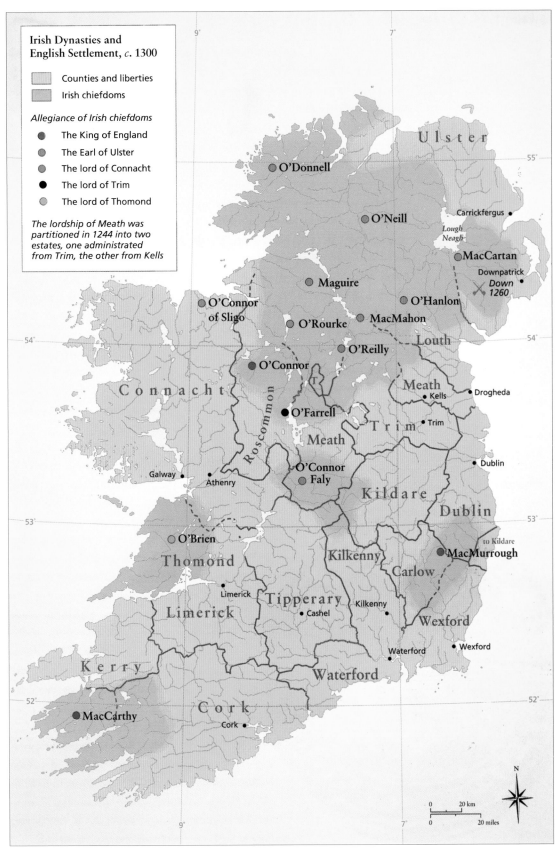

Irish Dynasties and
English Settlement, *c.* 1300

Counties and liberties
Irish chiefdoms

Allegiance of Irish chiefdoms
- The King of England
- The Earl of Ulster
- The lord of Connacht
- The lord of Trim
- The lord of Thomond

*The lordship of Meath was
partitioned in 1244 into two
estates, one administered
from Trim, the other from Kells*

U l s t e r

O'Donnell

O'Neill

Carrickfergus

Lough
Neagh

MacCartan

Downpatrick
*Down
1260*

Maguire

O'Connor
of Sligo

O'Hanlon

O'Rourke

MacMahon

O'Reilly

Louth

C o n n a c h t

O'Connor

Meath

Kells

Drogheda

O'Farrell

T r i m

Trim

Meath

Galway

Athenry

O'Connor
Faly

Dublin

Kildare

Dublin

O'Brien

to Kildare

Thomond

Kilkenny

MacMurrough

Carlow

Limerick

Limerick

Tipperary

Kilkenny

Cashel

Kilkenny

Wexford

Wexford

Waterford

K e r r y

Waterford

MacCarthy

C o r k

Waterford

Cork

N

0   20 km

0   20 miles

The Decline of English Power

THE INABILITY of the newcomers to uproot the most powerful Irish kings and the failure of greater numbers of English colonists to settle in Ireland ensured that a complete conquest of the island could not be speedily achieved.

However, the flame of ambition which had brought Strongbow and his kind to Ireland in 1170 continued to burn brightly, and as late as the 1230s a full-scale invasion of Connacht was launched which resulted in English colonies being established in places as remote as north Mayo.

That this impetus was not sustained was partly the consequence of many able English leaders in Ireland dying in the 1240s without leaving sons to succeed them. As a result, their estates were divided among daughters whose husbands often had no interest in Ireland and spent no time supporting or defending their holdings in the country. Violent quarrels broke out between the FitzGeralds and the de Burghs, the most important colonial families in the country, and even the suburbs of Dublin, the centre of the king of England's government in Ireland, was regularly attacked, from the 1270s onwards, by the MacMurroughs of the Wicklow Mountains. The colonial parliament of 1297 painted a gloomy picture of the situation and explicitly acknowledged, for the first time, that some of the settlers had begun to abandon their own culture and instead to embrace that of the native Irish.

The weaknesses of the colonial establishment were starkly revealed when Edward Bruce, brother of Robert I, king of Scotland, invaded Ulster in 1315 and joined with O'Neill in attempting to drive out the English settlers. Despite failing to gain unanimous Irish support, Bruce was able to beat English forces on several occasions and came close to capturing Dublin itself. It was not until 1318 that the Scottish menace was finally removed with the defeat and death of Bruce at Fochart near Dundalk.

It might be said, however, that the Bruce invasion also revealed the strength of the English presence in Ireland. The settlers were united in their opposition to the Scottish invaders, despite attempts by Bruce to woo or bully them from their allegiance to the king of England.

The image they had of themselves as a conquering people chosen by God to civilize the barbaric Irish remained as strong in 1320 as it had been a century-and-a-half earlier. If anything, the decline in their fortunes in the intervening period made them even more determined to survive.

Below: The Anglo-Irish victory at the Battle of Athenry in 1316 is commemorated in the seal of the town. The severed heads may represent the vanquished chieftains of Connacht. Five Irish kings are said to have died in this battle.

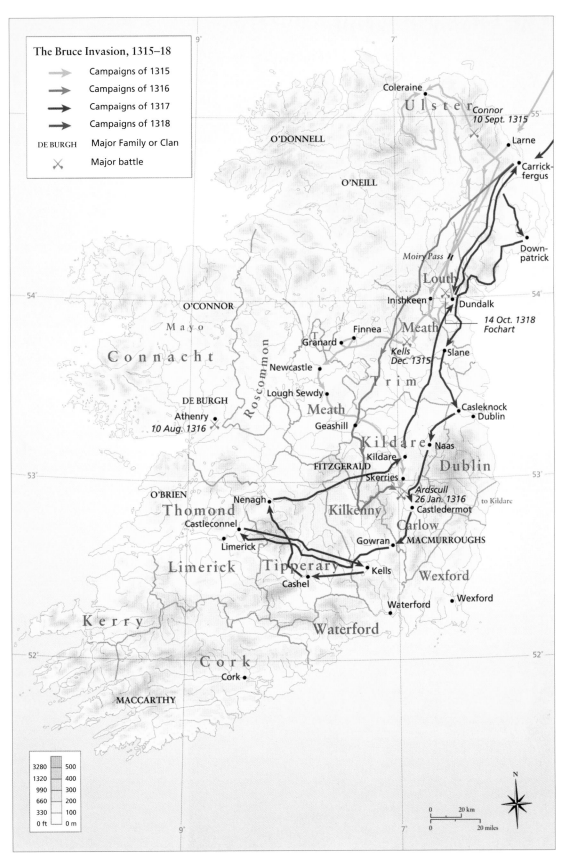

The Bruce Invasion, 1315–18

→ Campaigns of 1315
→ Campaigns of 1316
→ Campaigns of 1317
→ Campaigns of 1318
DE BURGH   Major Family or Clan
✕   Major battle

Coleraine

U l s t e r
Connor
10 Sept. 1315
✕

Larne

Carrick-
fergus

O'DONNELL

O'NEILL

Down-
patrick

Moiry Pass

L o u t h

O'CONNOR

Inishkeen
Dundalk

14 Oct. 1318
Fochart

M a y o

Finnea
M e a t h

✕

C o n n a c h t

Granard
Newcastle
Slane

Roscommon

Lough Sewdy
M e a t h

Kells
Dec. 1315

T r i m

DE BURGH

Casleknock
Dublin

Athenry
10 Aug. 1316
✕

Geashill

K i l d a r e   Naas

Kildare

D u b l i n

FITZGERALD
Skerries

O'BRIEN

Ardscull
26 Jan. 1316
Castledermot

to Kildare

Nenagh

T h o m o n d

K i l k e n n y

C a r l o w

Castleconnel

Gowran   MACMURROUGHS

Limerick

Kells

Cashel

T i p p e r a r y

W e x f o r d

L i m e r i c k

Wexford

K e r r y

Waterford

W a t e r f o r d

C o r k

Cork

MACCARTHY

3280   500
1320   400
990   300
660   200
330   100
0 ft   0 m

N

0   20 km

0   20 miles

The Gaelic Revival

THE VICTORY of the English over the Scots in 1318 did not end the problems of the colony. Ireland, which had once been an important source of revenue for the king of England was now a heavy drain on his resources, and the natural disasters of the 14th century — famine in 1315–17 and the Black Death in 1348–49 and regularly thereafter — weakened the Irish economy still further. The problems of landlord absenteeism and feuding between nobles increased apace, and large numbers of peasants and artisans migrated back to England in the face of Irish reconquest of frontier settlements.

The greatest threat posed to the English by the Irish, however, was cultural rather than military. Beginning with the Statutes of Kilkenny of 1366, futile attempts were made legally to prohibit the English from speaking the Irish language, marrying Irish partners or fostering children with Irish families. Such a defensive attitude was a testament to the strength and appeal of Gaelic culture. In the century after 1170 this culture had been in full retreat, but by the end of the 13th century confidence had returned and the educated families of Gaelic Ireland embarked on a 300-year period of tremendous energy in the production of poetry, legal commentaries, translations of European medical treatises and works of genealogy and Irish history.

The tone of much of this cultural revival was decidedly archaic. To give but one example, ways of inaugurating Irish kings which had disappeared but 'were remembered by the old men and recorded in the old books' were revived in the early 14th century. This emphasis on continuity with the pre-invasion past could not hide the enormous changes which had occurred in Gaelic society in the meantime. The Irish had not been slow to borrow from the English in matters such as warfare, architecture and law, while Irish kingship itself had become so degraded that by the end of the Middle Ages an Irish 'king' was no longer a law-giver with a public role sanctioned by the Church, but was rather the warrior head of the local dynasty who ensured his authority by billeting his troop of galloglass on the local population. Given the power which the culture of Gaelic Ireland permitted its leaders, it is perhaps not surprising that it should have appealed so strongly to leading colonial families like the de Burghs, Butlers and FitzGeralds.

Below: Rosserk, Co. Mayo, a Franciscan friary of the Third Order Regular, founded in the 15th century. This was a time of religious enthusiasm in Ireland. The Irish founded new monastic houses and went on pilgrimage as far afield as Santiago in Spain. Irish poets also produced quantities of religious verse of great beauty at this time.

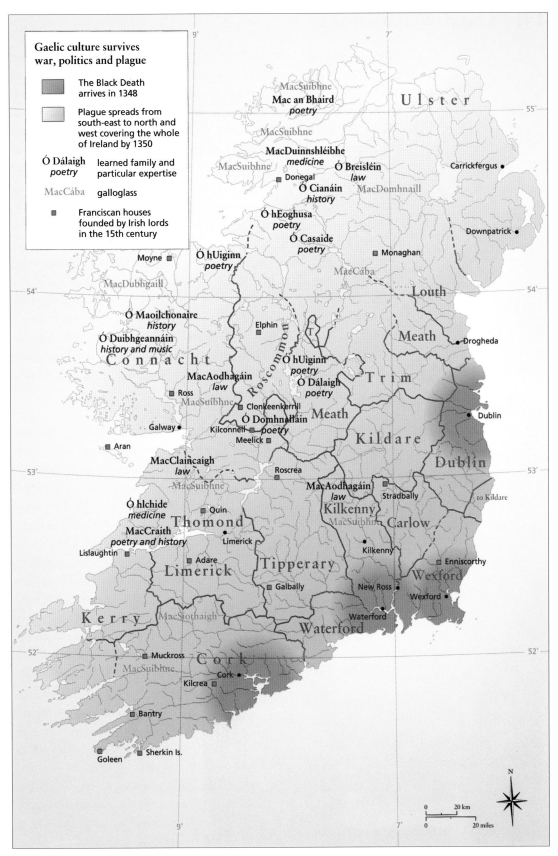

Gaelic culture survives war, politics and plague

The Black Death arrives in 1348

Plague spreads from south-east to north and west covering the whole of Ireland by 1350

Ó Dálaigh
poetry — learned family and particular expertise

MacCába — galloglass

■ Franciscan houses founded by Irish lords in the 15th century

MacSuibhne
Mac an Bhaird
poetry

U l s t e r

MacSuibhne

MacDuinnshléibhe
medicine

MacSuibhne

● Donegal

Ó Breisléin
law

Carrickfergus ●

Ó Cianáin
history

MacDomhnaill

Ó hEoghusa
poetry

Downpatrick ●

Ó Casaide
poetry

■ Monaghan

Moyne ■

Ó hUiginn
poetry

MacCába

MacDubhgaill

L o u t h

Ó Maoilchonaire
history

Elphin ●

M e a t h

Ó Duibhgeannáin
history and music

Drogheda ●

C o n n a c h t

Ó hUiginn
poetry

T r i m

MacAodhagáin
law

Ó Dálaigh
poetry

■ Ross

MacSuibhne

M e a t h

Clonkeenkerrill ■

Ó Domhnalláin
poetry

Galway ●

Kilconnell ■

K i l d a r e

Meelick ■

● Dublin

■ Aran

MacClaincaigh
law

Roscrea ●

D u b l i n

MacSuibhne

MacAodhagáin
law

Stradbally ●

to Kildare

Ó hIchide
medicine

● Quin

K i l k e n n y

C a r l o w

MacCraith
poetry and history

T h o m o n d

MacSuibhne

Lislaughtin ■

● Limerick

Kilkenny ●

Enniscorthy ■

■ Adare

T i p p e r a r y

W e x f o r d

L i m e r i c k

Galbally ■

New Ross ■

K e r r y

MacSíothaigh

Wexford ●

W a t e r f o r d

Waterford ●

■ Muckross

C o r k

■ Kilcrea

MacSuibhne

Cork ●

■ Bantry

■ Goleen   ■ Sherkin Is.

9°   7°

N

0   20 km
0   20 miles

45

The Late Middle Ages

Between 1360 and 1399 the English crown devoted an unusual amount of time and money to Ireland in an effort to shore up the position of the colonists there. Edward III's son Lionel of Clarence was chief governor for five years during the 1360s, and the next king of England, Richard II, came to Ireland twice in the 1390s. Richard was deposed in 1399 and his 15th-century successors were not prepared to throw any more money at the Irish problem. Instead the great magnate families, the Butlers in Ormond and the FitzGeralds in Desmond and Kildare, were expected to represent the crown's interests and defend the settlement. These magnates had long experience of dealing with the Irish of their own districts and they had taken on many of the characteristics of their neighbours. This was not to the liking of the settlers in the towns and those who dwelt in the area between Dublin and Dundalk which by the end of the century was known as the Pale. This group wished to remain as English as possible and they sent a constant stream of complaints about the earls to London. Allowing local magnates to rule, whatever its drawbacks, did bring stability to Ireland, and the amount of new building which took place in the 15th century suggests that it was a time of modest prosperity and economic growth.

When the settlers went to England they found themselves treated as foreigners, and their feeling of resentment showed through in 1460 when they declared in the Irish parliament that they were not bound by laws passed in parliament in England unless they passed them as well. This independent stance became a major problem after the victory of Henry Tudor over Richard III at Bosworth Field in 1485 when the earl of Kildare, who had supported Richard, used the Irish parliament to forward the claim of the pretender Lambert Simnel to the English throne. In 1494 Henry VII dispatched Sir Edward Poynings to bring the settlers to heel and in a parliament held at Drogheda late that year the chief governor pushed through legislation which restated categorically the subordinate position of the Irish to the English parliament. Kildare's stranglehold on real power in Ireland survived this setback, but his actions were in future monitored more closely, and his family was finally driven into rebellion and disgrace in 1534. There was to be no Irish solution to the Irish problem as a new era of English power dawned.

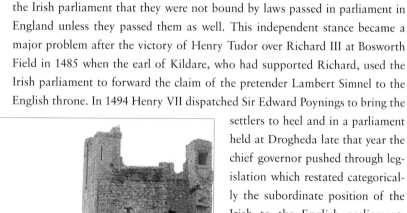

Below: *Tower-houses were the most notable development in Irish secular architecture in the late Middle Ages, and were built by both Anglo-Irish and native Irish lords. This one, at Leighlinbridge, Co. Carlow, is a 16th-century device for guarding a vital crossing of the River Barrow.*

Late medieval Ireland

O'Brien — Native Irish dynasties

Dalton — English names

⧄ areas obedient to England

— Pale, 1488

O'Doherty
MacDonnell
MacQuillan
MacSweeney
O'Cahan
O'Neill of Clandeboye
Carrickfergus
O'Donnell
The Great O'Neill
MacCartan
Savage
O'Neill of the Fews
Downpatrick
O'Rourke
Maguire
Magennis
O'Dowda
Sligo
MacMahon
O'Connor Sligo
Magauran
O'Hanlon
Barrett
MacRannell
MacDermot
O'Reilly
Dundalk
O'Connor Don and Rua
O'Farrall
MacCostello
O'Dempsey
Drogheda
MacWilliam Burke
O'Malley
Dalton
Bermingham
Dillon
O'Flaherty
O'Kelly
Maynooth
Clanricard Burke
O'Melaghlin
Dublin
Galway
MacGeoghegan
Athenry
O'Madden
O'Connor Faly
Earldom of Kildare
MacCoghlan
O'Toole
O'More
O'Dempsey
O'Brien
MacGillapatrick
O'Byrne
Wicklow
MacNamara
Earldom of Ormond
MacMurrough
Limerick
O'Mulryan
Clanwilliam Burke
Kilkenny
O'Connor Kerry
Earldom of Desmond
FitzMaurice
Waterford
Wexford
Le Poer
Roche
Condon
MacCarthy Mór
Barry
MacCarthy
Cork
O'Sullivan Mór
O'Sullivan Beare
MacCarthy Reagh
O'Mahony
O'Driscoll

3280	500
1320	400
990	300
660	200
330	100
0 ft	0 m

N

0   20 km

0   20 miles

The Growth of Dublin

Dublin takes its name from the Irish Duibhlinn, 'black pool', which possibly refers to a pool on the Poddle, a tributary of the river Liffey. Duibhlinn was an ecclesiastical centre seized in 841 by Vikings who had been ravaging Ireland for the previous half-century. The alternative Irish name for the city, Áth Cliath, 'the ford of the hurdles', explains its strategic significance, as it was one of the region's most important crossing-points.

Above: St Patrick's Cathedral, Dublin, 1793, by James Malton. The cathedral is shown here from the south-east and it is a valuable historical document as it shows a fine example of Early Gothic architecture in Ireland before the 19th-century restorations. St Patrick's pre-dated the English invasion, but the extant building was erected after it, and elevated to cathedral status c. 1220.

It quickly became the main Viking military base and trading centre in Ireland and its Norse, and sometimes Danish, rulers, involved themselves in raiding and military alliances in Ireland and abroad. In the first half of the 10th century members of its ruling family were also kings of York. In the course of time, though, Dublin became ever more closely integrated into Irish politics, and its Hiberno-Scandinavian rulers exercised power over its hinterland, a trace of which survives today in the area known as Fingal (*Fine Gall*, 'the territory of the foreigners').

Though a powerful military and naval force, the men of Dublin were defeated by the Munster king Brian Boru at the battle of Clontarf in 1014, and thereafter the town was largely an appanage claimed by the contenders for the elusive high-kingship of Ireland. By the time Ireland was invaded by the English in 1169, Dublin had come to replace Tara as the country's symbolic capital, and was also the single greatest concentration of economic wealth, with an extensive network of trading contacts overseas.

It fell to English arms in 1170, and when King Henry II visited the country in the following year he took the city, and what became County Dublin, into his own hands. Dublin remained the headquarters of the new English colony thereafter, Dublin Castle, which underwent many phases of fortification and expansion in the following centuries, coming to represent, in both a practical and symbolic way, the seat of English government in Ireland.

In the aftermath of the English invasion Dublin enjoyed an extended period of physical expansion (including the reclamation of lands from the Liffey), and of economic development and prosperity, as exemplified by the architectural splendour of its two medieval cathedrals, and the foundation of several wealthy religious houses. By the early 14th century, however, the city had begun to decline, in common with the experience elsewhere, though in Dublin's case it lasted until the 17th century. Growth on a considerable scale only gathered pace following the Restoration in 1660, and the 18th century was arguably the most colourful in the city's history, the arts and architecture in particular finding encouragement from the wealthy society of what was now regarded as the second city of the empire.

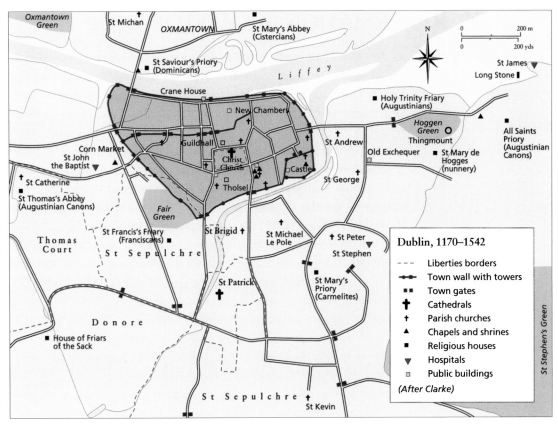

Dublin, 1170–1542

- - - - Liberties borders
●━■━● Town wall with towers
■ ■ Town gates
✝ Cathedrals
† Parish churches
▲ Chapels and shrines
■ Religious houses
▼ Hospitals
▫ Public buildings

(After Clarke)

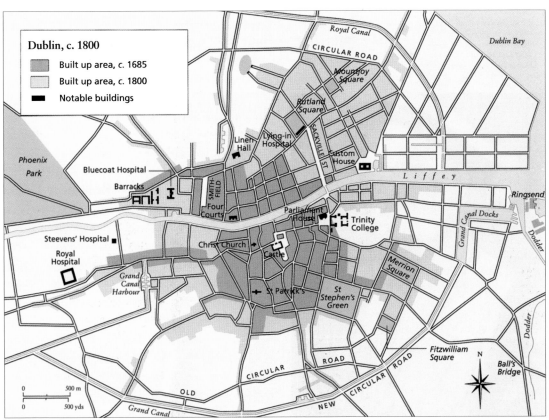

Dublin, c. 1800

▨ Built up area, *c.* 1685
▨ Built up area, *c.* 1800
■ Notable buildings

PART III: REFORMATION TO RESTORATION

*Colm Lennon
and
Raymond Gillespie*

BY THE END of Ireland's troubled 15th century, the English lordship of the island in practice extended over the eastern Pale region, east Munster, the towns and their hinterlands, and some scattered enclaves in the west and north. In an age of geographical expansion, Ireland became a zone of English colonial intervention and experimentation. The increasing transatlantic trade affected the thinly populated, lightly urbanized island only slowly. After the overthrow of dozens of local and regional lordships of Gaelic and Anglo-Norman origin, the political power of the English Crown became centralized in Dublin by about 1600. While the two ethnic communities of late medieval Ireland were not mutually exclusive and shared social and economic ties, their group identities were defined against English newcomers, some of whom characterized the native people pejoratively in their writings.

The genesis of the Tudors' commitment to positive policies for Ireland lay in England's increasingly complex entanglement in European diplomacy. As relations with France, the Empire and Spain deteriorated, English concern about the fragility of Ireland's defences against continental invasion grew. The Reformation reached Ireland as part of Henry VIII's programme of breaking with the papacy and chaining Church and state institutions more tightly to the monarchy. In that context the raising of Ireland in 1541 to the constitutional status of a kingdom was another assertion of royal power in the face of Roman claims that the country was a papal fief.

The kingship of Ireland was more importantly the centrepiece of a programme of political and social reform designed to overhaul the Irish adminstration and to restructure the Gaelic and gaelicized lordships, bringing them into line with English norms. Originally conceived as a potential partnership of the communities within a unified constitutional framework, the putative kingdom never became a reality. In the absence of a monarch, the later Tudor viceroys attempted to persuade the native lords to accept English political relationships, common law and land tenure. But persuasion was interspersed with bouts of intimidation and with plantation ventures settling newcomers on lands to which the Crown claimed title. Resistance to English officials' increasingly forceful efforts to impose new institutions resulted in revolts in all provinces, culminating in the struggle of the Nine Years War centred on Ulster. The breakdown of trust between the earl of Tyrone and the English authorities was symptomatic of the tense situation at the end of the century, leading to a hugely

Below: Henry VIII of England during whose reign (1509–47) the Reformation began in Ireland and under whom Ireland was raised to the status of kingdom in 1541.

Below: Ireland engraved by Van den Keere, in England in 1591, published by Hondius. More accurate than the well known Ortelius map published a year later. This is reproduced from one of only two surviving copies.

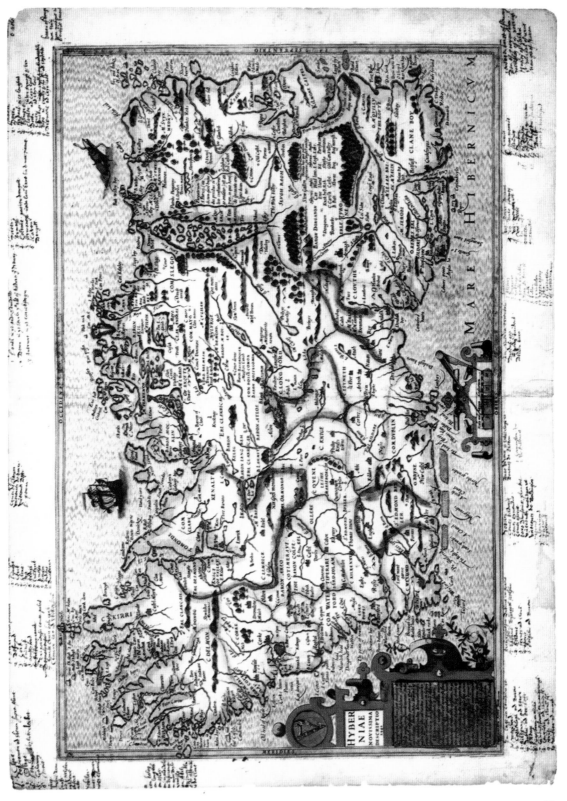

Right: *Upon the death of Mary in 1558, Elizabeth became Queen of England. During her reign, English rule was gradually extended into all four provinces of Ireland, but the Protestant Reformation failed to win more than a small following.*

Right: *Until the early 17th century Gaelic society in many regions of Ireland remained relatively unaffected by the policy of anglicization. Eventually, however, the power of the Gaelic chieftains and their cultural and social practices succumbed to the influence of newly-settled officials and planters.*

expensive campaign in which the Spanish monarchy intervened.

The Tudor conquest of Ireland by 1603 had come about largely as a response to rebellions throughout the island. The succeeding Stuart administration seized the opportunity for further colonization in Ulster after the pivotal event of the flight of the Earls in 1607. The central institutions of the state were in theory now effective throughout the land. The New English community comprising recently-arrived Protestant officials, planters and ecclesiastics asserted its rights to be considered the ruling class in place of the Old English élite. The members of the latter group, while not manifesting overt disloyalty, had become increasingly disenchanted with the government's political, fiscal and religious policies. For the most part they failed to respond to the state Church's lacklustre evangelical campaign in

support of the Reformation, instead finding their spiritual home in the European Counter-Reformation. This movement also animated key sections of the Gaelic population, some of whose leaders managed to adapt to the new political and economic realities. Most, however, lost ground to the more thrusting and entrepreneurial New English settlers.

Above: *William of Orange, later King William III of England, initially unenthusiastic about his involvement in Ireland, was drawn there by the presence of his rival James II. After defeating James at the Battle of the Boyne on 1 July 1690, he, like James, left Ireland never to return.*

The absolutist Stuart regime of the 1630s came into conflict with the parliamentary side when Ireland became enmeshed in the 1640s in the severe constitutional turbulence of the three kingdoms. The Cromwellian regime of the 1650s effected far-reaching landholding and political changes before the Restoration of the monarchy in 1660. The firmly Protestant governing establishment faced another massive challenge to its political and religious foundations in the form of the Jacobite takeover. Once this threat was removed the response of the élite was to frame the penal legislation to defend their religion and property. After the confiscations and plantations of the previous century, the preponderance of Irish land was now owned by the new Protestant élite which presided over rapid economic growth in agriculture and manufacturing.

In town and country, the old élites had been ousted from political and economic power and distanced by the Reformation from the Crown. The Restoration represented the triumph of the new Protestant colonial class which aspired to political, social and economic ascendancy in 18th-century Ireland.

The Protestant Reformation

THE REFORMATION was introduced into an Irish Church containing divisions similar to those in the socio-political sphere. While ecclesiastical institutions and practices among the Anglo-Irish were akin to those in much of pre-Reformation Europe, the Gaelic Church with its hereditary clerical families differed from its counterparts elsewhere. As in England, Henry VIII's legislation for royal supremacy in 1536 was the nub of a state-sponsored reform which oversaw the closure of religious houses under English jurisdiction. While Henry VIII's phase of the Reformation to 1547 was accomplished within a framework of conciliatory political reforms, the introduction thereafter of Protestant doctrines without local parliamentary sanction met with popular resistance. Consequently Mary's restoration of Catholicism engendered little opposition from a population which included only a small coterie of native Protestants.

When Elizabeth's parliament of 1560 legislated for an Anglican state Church, the government proceeded circumspectly with the minimum of coercion. In the absence of material resources for the educating and supporting of ministers, even in the heartland of the English Pale, and with few incentives for lay conversions to Protestantism such as were available in the era of monastic dissolutions, the élite in town and countryside where the Reformation was actually preached remained aloof from state Church services. They preferred to worship in the old mode in their homes and to conserve their ecclesiastical temporalities for the later endowment of continentally-trained Catholic priests. Further alienation of the older communities from the state religion occurred as it became increasingly identified with a harsh military regime in all provinces. In the 1590s, Trinity College, later to become known as the University of Dublin, was founded as a Reformation seminary and emerged as the centre of organized Protestant evangelism. Meanwhile, however, the Roman Church's Council of Trent of 1545, dominated by Italian and Spanish bishops, had met in three sessions over eighteen years and firmly established a new Catholic orthodoxy. By 1600, its 'Tridentine mission' had gained the allegiance of the majority of Ireland's Old English community. The appeal to faith and fatherland which emanated from the Ulster confederate leaders during the Nine Years War as they sought European Catholic assistance did not, however, find an echo among those loyal to the Crown. Nevertheless New English Protestants were distrustful of such 'half-subjects' and prepared to consolidate themselves into a small Protestant elect who were increasingly identifiable as the political and economic beneficiaries of the Tudor conquest.

Below: *Seminaries founded on the continent supplied Catholic priests for the Irish mission. Franciscan priest, Luke Wadding, was one of the foremost supporters of the Catholic cause in Ireland, composing spiritual texts as well as lobbying for political and financial support.*

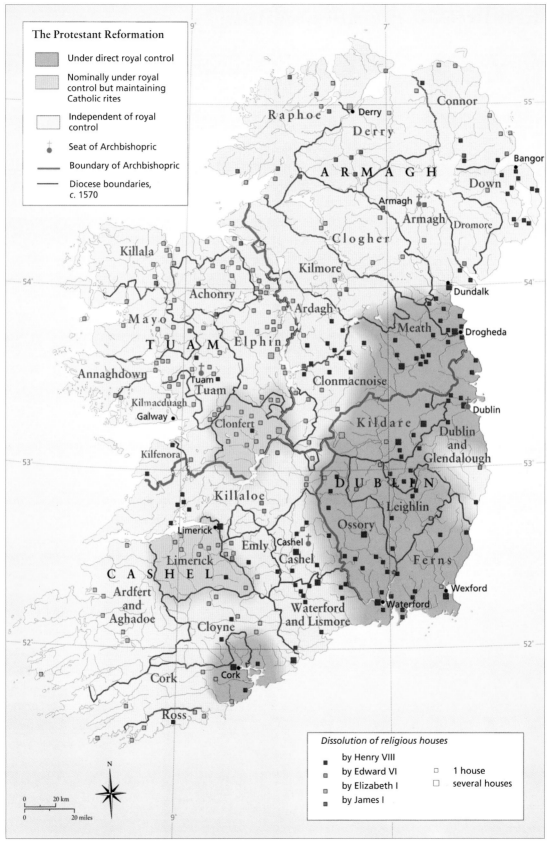

The Protestant Reformation

- Under direct royal control
- Nominally under royal control but maintaining Catholic rites
- Independent of royal control
- † Seat of Archbishopric
- Boundary of Archbishopric
- Diocese boundaries, c. 1570

Raphoe
Derry
Derry
Connor
ARMAGH
Bangor
Down
Armagh
Armagh
Dromore
Clogher
Killala
Kilmore
Achonry
Ardagh
Dundalk
Mayo
Meath
Drogheda
TUAM
Elphin
Annaghdown
Clonmacnoise
Tuam
Tuam
Kilmacduagh
Dublin
Galway
Clonfert
Kildare
Dublin and Glendalough
Kilfenora
DUBLIN
Killaloe
Leighlin
Limerick
Ossory
Limerick
Emly
Cashel
Ferns
CASHEL
Cashel
Ardfert and Aghadoe
Wexford
Cloyne
Waterford and Lismore
Waterford
Cork
Cork
Ross

N

0   20 km
0   20 miles

Dissolution of religious houses
- by Henry VIII
- by Edward VI   □ 1 house
- by Elizabeth I   □ several houses
- by James I

Elizabethan Administration

Above: *Ladies from the region of the Pale are shown here with mercenary soldiers from outside the Pale known as 'Kerns', warriors armed in the traditional Irish fashion. These illustrations were meant to contrast the civilization of the Pale with the supposed barbarism of the Gaelic west.*

THE ELIZABETHAN administration was the principal agency of the anglicization of the newly-constituted kingdom of Ireland. Its central institutions in Dublin underwent reform, although parliament met only three times during the reign. Under a succession of ambitious chief governors, the privy council was streamlined, becoming a more sophisticated and efficient executive body. The judiciary and exchequer were also overhauled, and new prerogative and ecclesiastical courts were established, those of Castle Chamber and High Commission. The huge costs of the reform programme rapidly outstripped available revenues, necessitating heavier taxation of the loyal Old English. Although co-existing uneasily with newly-arrived officials, this community, residing mostly in Leinster, grew increasingly resentful, as attested by its leaders' opposition strategy in parliament over a variety of constitutional, economic and religious issues.

Some progress was made by expanding the administration into the provinces, incorporating presidency councils to foster common law, tenurial reform, abolition of overlordship and of the oppressive and arbitrary taxation known as coign and livery. The key principle was conciliation through composition, a commuting of all levies into a compound tax payable mainly to the Crown, with small residual dues to former overlords. The latter would abandon fiscal and military autonomy, and instead come to rely on the judicial and security powers of the local president. He was to rule in the manner of the lord president of Wales or the Council of the North in England. At the same time, formerly Gaelic territories became shires, leading to the insertion of sheriffs and the establishment of English-style social and landholding structures.

Whereas in Munster the presidency system broke down as a result of revolts caused by displaced Irish swordsmen, aggressive English seneschals and widespread martial law and violence, in Connacht there was attempted a comprehensive settlement known as the Composition of Connacht. This settled the landholding pattern, particularly in the south of the province, establishing an income for the presidents and conciliar courts to redress the grievances of the principal lords. But lack of consistency in English policy was most detrimental in northern Connacht and in Ulster, where peaceful reform collapsed dramatically in the 1590s.

Below: *The citizens of Dublin turn out to greet and pay homage to Sir Henry Sidney, Lord Deputy of Ireland, on his victorious return from his campaigns against the Gaelic Irish in 1575, from John Derricke's* Image of Ireland, 1581.

O Sydney worthy of tryple re-
nowne,
For playing the naytours that
troubled the crowne. 1581

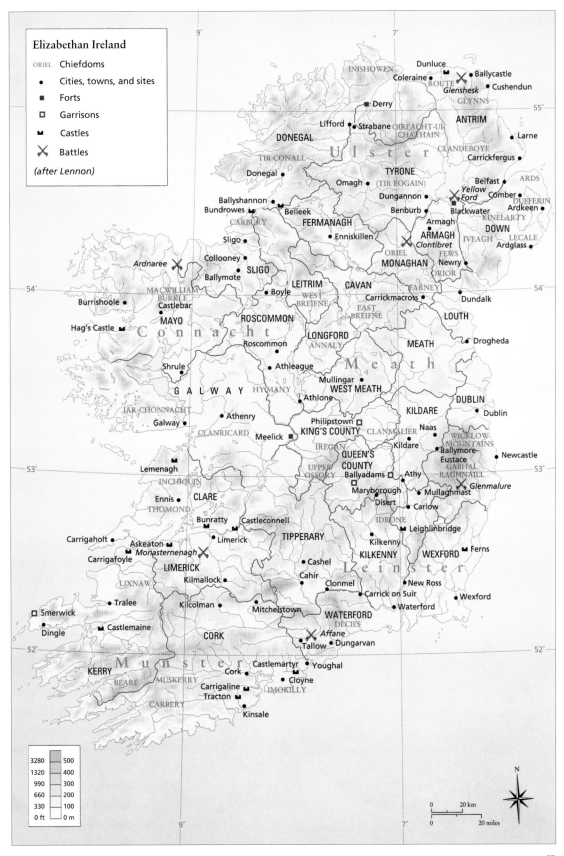

Elizabethan Ireland

ORIEL Chiefdoms
• Cities, towns, and sites
■ Forts
□ Garrisons
⌂ Castles
✕ Battles

(after Lennon)

Plantation and Resistance

ALTHOUGH mooted earlier in the 16th century, plantation of Irish lands by newcomers was not actually attempted until the 1550s in Laois and Offaly. Designed principally to secure the seized estates of the rebellious O'Mores and O'Connors on the Pale borders, the settlement of soldier-farmers in what became Queen's and King's Counties did not effect peaceful agricultural and civic conditions for many years. Some natives received lands in the plantation, but others, excluded from a stake, persisted in raiding the new settlements.

Private plantations were attempted in south-west Munster and parts of Ulster in the mid-Elizabethan years. The Newry settlement by the Bagenals evolved into a sound proprietorship, but the efforts of Sir Thomas Smith in the Ards and of the Earl of Essex in Antrim failed disastrously; they were vigorously opposed by Sir Brian O'Neill of Clandeboye, whose title was overridden by the newly-arrived Englishmen. Ensuing assassinations and massacres reflected the widespread resentment stirred up. In the barony of Idrone in Leinster the Butler family and their allies revolted against the land speculator Sir Peter Carew.

The relative failure of private entrepreneurs ensured a thorough state-planned enterprise in Munster after the collapse of the Earl of Desmond's revolt. After a hasty survey of the escheated estates in five counties, the London government allotted 300,000 acres to 35 undertakers, principally English gentlemen, courtiers and servitors. Recipients of estates of from 4,000 to 12,000 acres, the undertakers were to foster agrarian innovation, exploit natural resources, build substantial residences, encourage crafts and attract up to 90 families to work the land.

Some undertakers became absentees, but those who stayed faced many difficulties. Some lands were not free of putative owners who claimed to be freeholders rather than tenants-at-will of the late Earl, and others were burdened with debts and mortgages. Commissions were established to settle the claims of litigants, but proceedings were complex.

Below: This map shows the Laois-Offaly region in exceptional detail as part of the movement towards its plantation, the first large-scale English settlement in Ireland since the early stages of the Anglo-Norman invasion.

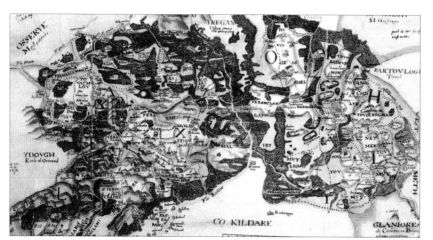

By the time of a major rebellion in 1598 and during the Nine Years War, the number of settlers was only about a third of that anticipated and the tentative roots of the fledgling colony could not withstand the avenging warbands and armies of Gaelic and Old English former landholders.

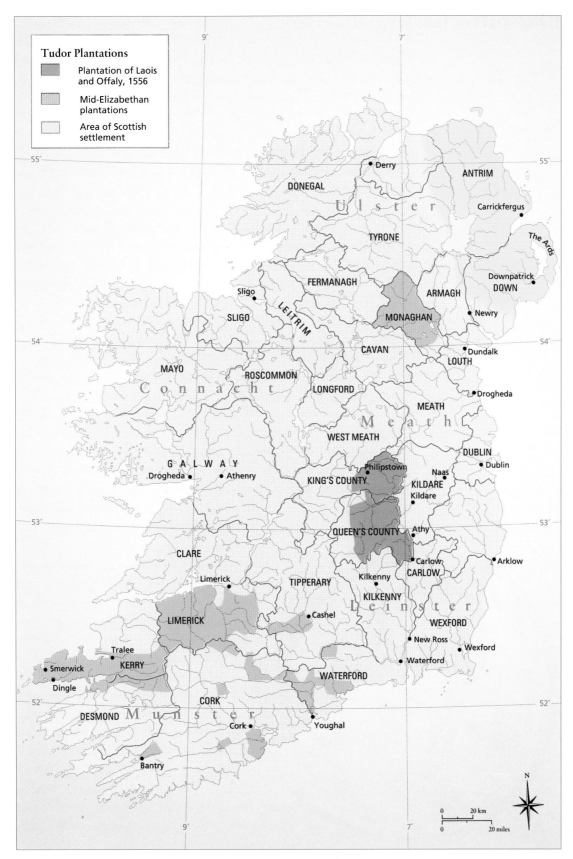

Tudor Plantations

- Plantation of Laois and Offaly, 1556
- Mid-Elizabethan plantations
- Area of Scottish settlement

O'Neill's Rising

WHEN HUGH O'NEILL, earl of Tyrone, took the field at Clontibret as leader of the Ulster insurgent confederacy in 1595, he resolved a long-standing dilemma. Having emerged as head of the powerful O'Neill dynasty after a fractious struggle, the erstwhile protégé of the government had to choose between heading an English-style administration in Ulster, thereby alienating his Gaelic kinsfolk, or throwing in his lot with the younger provincial leaders such as Hugh Roe O'Donnell and Hugh Maguire in their campaign against the infiltration of their territories by English officials. Having committed himself to the latter course, he unveiled a professionally-trained and well-equipped army which defended the approaches to the north against advancing English armies and scored many victories, culminating in the rout of the forces of his old antagonist, Henry Bagenal, at the Battle of the Yellow Ford in 1598.

Below: Hugh O'Neill, earl of Tyrone, was brought up among English settlers in the Irish midlands and fought on the side of the English in Munster and Ulster. Aspiring to a leadership role in central Ulster, he realized that the spread of English administration into the province represented a challenge to his position. Eventually he opted to head the confederacy of Ulster chieftains who had begun a major campaign against English garrisons and officials in Ulster in 1594. Aided by a disciplined army, he achieved many successes in the war to 1599. Thereafter the English under Mountjoy asserted their supremacy despite the landing of Spanish troops in Kinsale in 1601. The ensuing treaty of Mellifont guaranteed O'Neill's headship of his clan and his title to the earldom but pressure from officials in Dublin caused him to flee Ireland in 1607.

Now at the height of his success, O'Neill extended the war into the other provinces and renewed a quest for continental aid. As part of his campaign to enlist the support of the Old English in the Pale and in the towns, the earl issued articles demanding liberty of conscience for all the inhabitants of Ireland. Although unsuccessful in this bid, O'Neill and his allies caused the discomfiture of the earl of Essex's huge army in 1599. With the arrival of Lord Mountjoy as governor in 1600, the massive English resources committed to the quelling of the revolt began to bear fruit. By using scorched earth tactics, suborning disaffected confederates, and establishing a garrison near Derry, Mountjoy appeared to be undermining O'Neill's campaign when a Spanish fleet containing 3,500 troops arrived at Kinsale in 1601.

After a gruelling mid-winter march by O'Neill and O'Donnell and their assault on the English armies blockading Kinsale, the fateful engagement took place on Christmas Eve 1601, with the comprehensive defeat of the Irish allies while the Spanish remained at their base. Thereafter, O'Neill, under increasing pressure back in Ulster from Mountjoy's garrisons, eventually gave up his guerrilla war and signed a peace treaty at Mellifont in March 1603. The terms agreed were generous, O'Neill retaining his lands and earldom but relinquishing overlordship of traditional O'Neill vassals except O'Cahan. But four years later, the earl felt so threatened by newcomers that, along with his family and retainers, and like-minded lords, he fled to the continent.

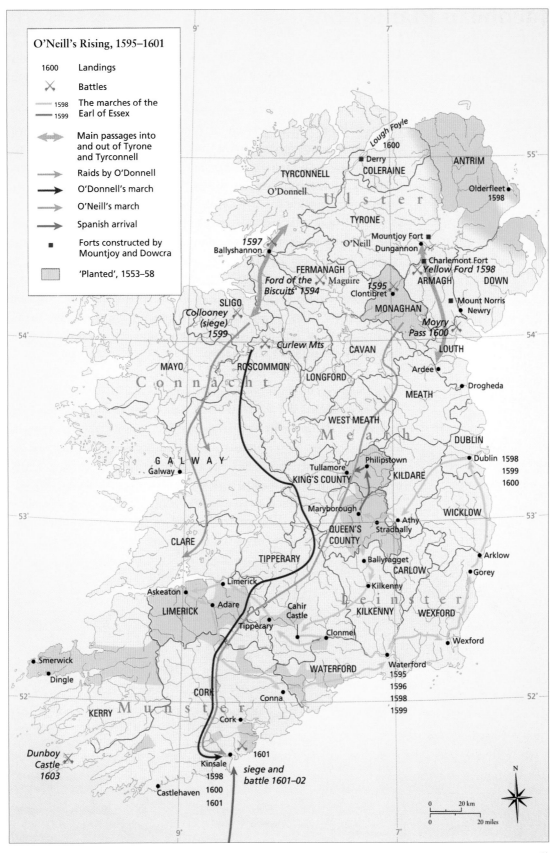

O'Neill's Rising, 1595–1601

1600	Landings
✗	Battles
—— 1598	The marches of the
—— 1599	Earl of Essex
⬌	Main passages into and out of Tyrone and Tyrconnell
→	Raids by O'Donnell
→	O'Donnell's march
→	O'Neill's march
→	Spanish arrival
■	Forts constructed by Mountjoy and Dowcra
	'Planted', 1553–58

Lough Foyle
1600
Derry
TYRCONNELL
COLERAINE
ANTRIM
U l s t e r
O'Donnell
Olderfleet
1598
TYRONE
Mountjoy Fort
O'Neill
Dungannon
1597
Ballyshannon
Charlemont Fort
Yellow Ford 1598
FERMANAGH
Ford of the
Biscuits' 1594
Maguire
1595
Clontibret
ARMAGH
DOWN
SLIGO
MONAGHAN
Mount Norris
Newry
Collooney
(siege)
1599
Moyry
Pass 1600
Curlew Mts
CAVAN
LOUTH
MAYO
ROSCOMMON
Ardee
C o n n a c h t
LONGFORD
Drogheda
MEATH
WEST MEATH
M e a t h
DUBLIN
GALWAY
Galway
Tullamore
KING'S COUNTY
Philipstown
KILDARE
Dublin 1598
1599
1600
Maryborough
WICKLOW
QUEEN'S
COUNTY
Athy
Stradbally
L e i n s t e r
CLARE
Arklow
TIPPERARY
Ballyragget
CARLOW
Gorey
Limerick
Kilkenny
Askeaton
Adare
Cahir
Castle
KILKENNY
WEXFORD
LIMERICK
Tipperary
Clonmel
Wexford
Smerwick
Waterford
Waterford
1595
Dingle
WATERFORD
1596
1598
1599
CORK
Conna
M u n s t e r
KERRY
Cork
Dunboy
Castle
1603
Kinsale
siege and
battle 1601–02
1601
1598
Castlehaven
1600
1601

N

0   20 km
0   20 miles

Jacobean Plantations

ON 3 SEPTEMBER 1607 some Ulster lords, recently restored to their lands after the Nine Years War, left Ireland from Lough Swilly without royal permission. Having relinquished their allegiance to the king, James I, their lands, comprising the modern counties of Armagh, Cavan, Donegal, Fermanagh, Derry and Tyrone, were escheated by the Crown. The event was unexpected and it took some time to provide an appropriate response. In January 1608 a plan for these counties was published involving a plantation similar to that of 16th-century Munster. Four groups were eligible for the Ulster lands: Scots and English settlers, servitors (royal officials), 'deserving' Irish and the Church. Baronies were set aside for the first three groups, who were to be granted estates ranging in size from 1,000 to 2,000 acres. The settler landlords were to introduce English and Scottish tenants onto these estates and effect improvements such as the building of towns. In 1610 County Coleraine was exempted from the scheme; the settlement there was to be carried out by a group of London livery companies and as a result the name of the county changed to Londonderry.

In the short term the impact of the plantation was much less than expected by government. Settlers did not arrive in the anticipated numbers and the social backgrounds of the landlords meant they had difficulty raising capital to improve the estates. Surveys in 1611, 1614 and 1622 provided evidence that settlers neither fulfilled their building obligations nor removed the native Irish from their lands. Much of the original settlement was destroyed by the 1641 rising.

In addition to the Ulster plantation there were smaller Jacobean settlements in counties Wexford, Longford and Leitrim, which, being mainly redistributions of land, did not require the introduction of settlers.

Right: *The town of Derry was granted to the corporations of the City of London in 1613, as part of the Jacobean plantations becoming, in the process, Londonderry. This drawing was made approximately 70 years later and shows Londonderry around 1680.*

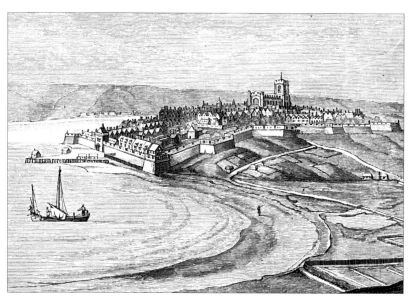

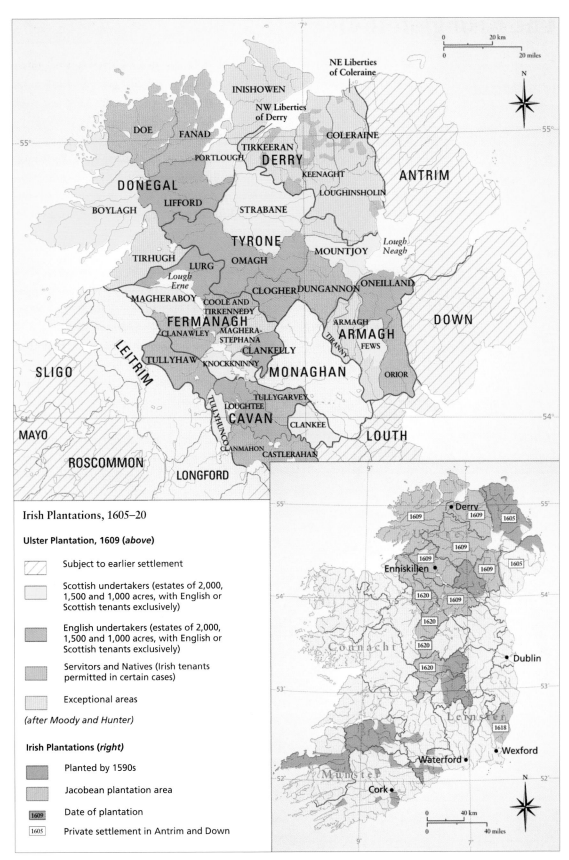

Irish Plantations, 1605–20

Ulster Plantation, 1609 (above)

Subject to earlier settlement

Scottish undertakers (estates of 2,000, 1,500 and 1,000 acres, with English or Scottish tenants exclusively)

English undertakers (estates of 2,000, 1,500 and 1,000 acres, with English or Scottish tenants exclusively)

Servitors and Natives (Irish tenants permitted in certain cases)

Exceptional areas

(after Moody and Hunter)

Irish Plantations (right)

Planted by 1590s

Jacobean plantation area

Date of plantation

Private settlement in Antrim and Down

The Rising of 1641

ON THE EVENING of 22 October 1641 a group of Ulstermen of native stock, under the command of Sir Phelim O'Neill, seized Charlemont Castle. They claimed not to be in rebellion against the king but took arms to protect his rights against 'evil counsellors' and even produced a forged royal commission to vindicate their action. The military campaign pushed south, arriving at Drogheda in December 1641. This military pressure forced the Catholic Old English of the Pale to join the war, but their constitutional instinct led them to establish a representative assembly, the Confederation of Kilkenny, to negotiate a settlement with the Dublin government.

The outbreak of civil war in England in 1642 added a further complication to the Irish situation: the king, Charles I, wanted peace in Ireland so that he could use Irish troops in England. The situation was further internationalized by the arrival of a force of Irishmen from the Spanish Netherlands under the command of Owen Roe O'Neill and Scots commanded by Robert Munroe in 1642. War dragged on for two years until a cessation was declared in September 1643 to

S:r Phillom O Cheife Traytor   *Neale of all Ireland*

enable a peace to be negotiated between the Confederates and the Lord Lieutenant, the earl of Ormond. This proved divisive within the settler camp, and a number of military commanders appealed to the English Parliamentarians for support. The first attempt at a treaty, the Ormond peace of August 1646, proved divisive within the Confederation, the Papal Nuncio Giovanni Rinuccini claiming there were not enough guarantees for the Catholic church. The landing of a Parliamentary force in Ireland in 1647 and plans for the second civil war in England drew together the pro-peace confederates, who negotiated a second treaty in January 1647. After the execution of Charles I on 30 January, this formed the basis of an alliance between the Confederates and the Dublin government against the power of the English Parliamentarians. Thus the Irish civil war became an extension of the English civil war, which was not concluded until 1653.

Left: *Sir Phelim O'Neill, leader of a group of Catholic landowners, decided to strengthen their claim to special consideration by armed revolt against the English government of Ireland.*

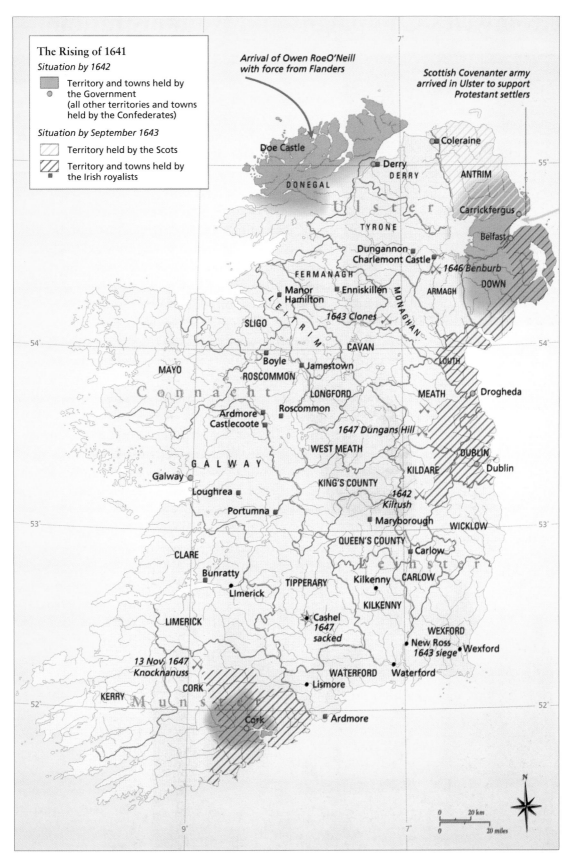

The Rising of 1641

Situation by 1642

- Territory and towns held by the Government (all other territories and towns held by the Confederates)

Situation by September 1643

- Territory held by the Scots
- Territory and towns held by the Irish royalists

Arrival of Owen Roe O'Neill with force from Flanders

Scottish Covenanter army arrived in Ulster to support Protestant settlers

Doe Castle

Coleraine

Derry

DERRY

ANTRIM

DONEGAL

Carrickfergus

Belfast

U l s t e r

TYRONE

Dungannon

Charlemont Castle

1646 Benburb

DOWN

FERMANAGH

Manor Hamilton

Enniskillen

ARMAGH

MONAGHAN

SLIGO

1643 Clones

LEITRIM

CAVAN

LOUTH

MAYO

Boyle

Jamestown

ROSCOMMON

C o n n a c h t

LONGFORD

MEATH

Drogheda

Ardmore

Castlecoote

Roscommon

1647 Dungans Hill

WEST MEATH

DUBLIN

Dublin

GALWAY

KILDARE

Galway

KING'S COUNTY

Loughrea

1642

Kilrush

Portumna

Maryborough

WICKLOW

QUEEN'S COUNTY

L e i n s t e r

CLARE

Carlow

Bunratty

Kilkenny

CARLOW

Limerick

TIPPERARY

KILKENNY

LIMERICK

Cashel

1647

sacked

WEXFORD

New Ross

1643 siege

Wexford

13 Nov. 1647

Knocknanuss

WATERFORD

Waterford

CORK

Lismore

KERRY

M u n s t e r

Cork

Ardmore

N

0   20 km

0   20 miles

Cromwell's Campaigns and Administration

Above: *Oliver Cromwell, ruthless general, country gentleman, devoted father and Puritan zealot. He came to Ireland determined to stamp out military resistance to government authority, to wreak vengeance for the supposed massacres of 1641, and to convert the entire population to the Protestant faith.*

Below: *The illustration features Burntcourt (Clogheen), Co. Tipperary, a plantation mansion which had only been newly built in 1650 when it was burnt by its owner's wife to deny it to the approaching Cromwellians.*

THE EXECUTION of Charles I on 30 January 1649 united the previously divided Irish supporters of the king. The establishment of a Royalist bastion close to England necessitated intervention by the Parliamentary forces. A Parliamentarian army was already in Ireland and had won a significant victory at Baggot Rath (Rathmines) in 1649. That August it was strengthened by a well supplied and trained force under the command of Oliver Cromwell, and this highly-organized and experienced army then quickly gained control of most of the country. Key east-coast walled towns, such as Drogheda in September, and Waterford in December, were taken using cannon, which had been little used in the 1640s. By May 1650 Cromwell had left Ireland for the Scottish campaign, leaving Henry Ireton as his deputy to conclude the war, and by 1651 west-coast towns like Limerick and Galway were under Parliamentary control. The war was over by April 1653.

The government of Ireland between 1651 and 1654 was under the control of Parliamentary commissioners who were also military officers. In 1654 one of these, Charles Fleetwood, was appointed to the civilian office of Lord Deputy, and in 1657 he was replaced by Oliver Cromwell's second son Henry. Henry Cromwell shifted the power-base of the government away from the army and instead conciliated the older political élites, especially the northern Presbyterians and the Munster Protestants.

The 1650s saw a number of significant innovations: the Irish parliament was abolished and replaced by a less than adequate Irish representation at the Westminster parliament; the legal system was made more efficient; and educational institutions such as Trinity College, Dublin were developed to train a reliable and godly ministry.

In December 1659, the Cromwellian regime collapsed as a result of an army coup and in May 1660 Charles II was proclaimed king in Dublin.

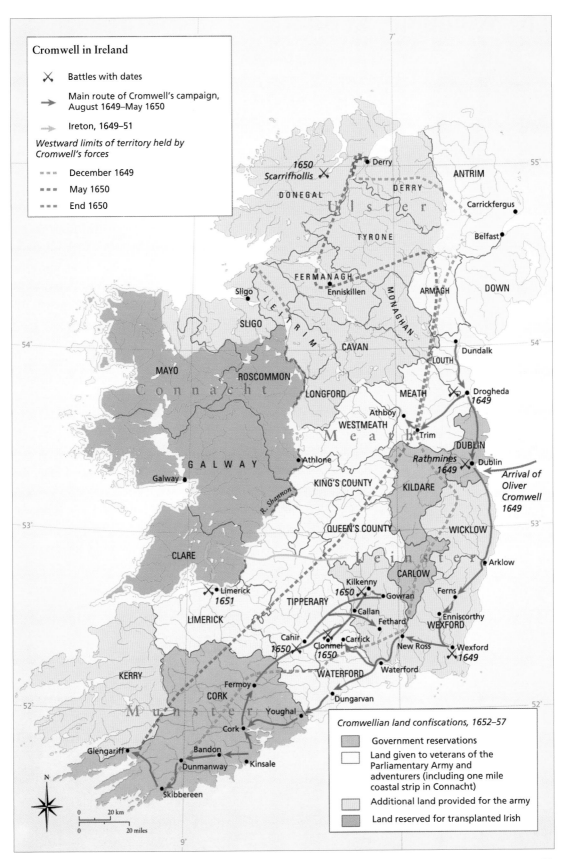

Cromwell in Ireland

✕ Battles with dates

➤ Main route of Cromwell's campaign, August 1649–May 1650

➤ Ireton, 1649–51

Westward limits of territory held by Cromwell's forces

╍╍╍ December 1649

━━━ May 1650

▬▬▬ End 1650

Cromwellian land confiscations, 1652–57

Government reservations

Land given to veterans of the Parliamentary Army and adventurers (including one mile coastal strip in Connacht)

Additional land provided for the army

Land reserved for transplanted Irish

The Williamite Revolution

Above: A medal struck to commemorate the Protestant victories, 1690–91.

WHEN THE Catholic King James II came to the throne in 1685 there was some nervousness among Irish Protestants. James tried to reassure them with the appointment of a Protestant Lord Deputy, Lord Clarendon. Clarendon's recall in 1687 and the appointment of the earl of Tyrconnell signalled the beginning of a more pro-Catholic policy in Ireland with the Catholicization of the army and local government. While Tyrconnell wished to undo the land settlement of the 1660s, James was more cautious. The birth of a royal heir in June 1688 caused alarm among the English political élite, who invited James's son-in-law William of Orange to take the English throne, whereupon James fled London for France.

The political situation worsened in 1688, when economic difficulties, combined with political opportunism, led to local disturbances. Memories of the 1641 rising were revived and some Protestants fled to England. Most, however, counselled caution, and in December 1688 the closing of the gates of Derry against the army of the Jacobite earl of Antrim was regarded by many as folly. James landed in Ireland with French support in March 1689 and summoned parliament in June. It was this parliament, with its proposal for the dismantling of the Restoration land settlement, which finally alienated James from any residual Protestant support.

William III had been reluctant to come to Ireland, but James's presence and the European implications of the French presence there obligated him. His forces arrived in Ulster in August 1689 and William followed almost a year later. He marched south and engaged James's army at the Boyne on 1 July. Following his defeat, James fled to France while William pushed his campaign west before leaving Ireland in September 1690. The war was concluded by the Treaty of Limerick, after a siege of that city, in October 1691.

Right: At the end of the second siege of Limerick the Jacobites surrendered, signing the Treaty of Limerick in 1691. As a result of the surrender, many thousands of Catholic officers and soldiers left Ireland to join the armies of France. They became known as the 'wild geese' and were reinforced in the following hundred years by tens of thousands of their countrymen.

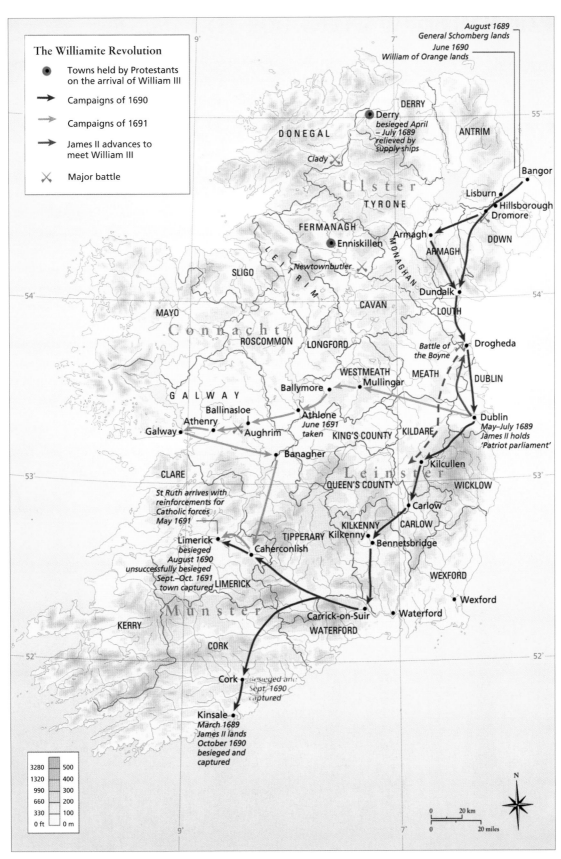

The Williamite Revolution

- ● Towns held by Protestants on the arrival of William III
- → Campaigns of 1690
- → Campaigns of 1691
- → James II advances to meet William III
- ✕ Major battle

August 1689
General Schomberg lands
June 1690
William of Orange lands

DERRY

Derry
besieged April
– July 1689
relieved by
supply ships

DONEGAL

ANTRIM

Clady ✕

U l s t e r

TYRONE

Bangor

Lisburn

Hillsborough
Dromore

DOWN

FERMANAGH

● Enniskillen

Armagh ●

ARMAGH

MONAGHAN

L
E
I
T
R
I
M

Newtownbutler ✕

SLIGO

Dundalk ●

LOUTH

MAYO

C o n n a c h t

CAVAN

ROSCOMMON

LONGFORD

Battle of
the Boyne ✕

Drogheda

WESTMEATH

MEATH

DUBLIN

Mullingar

Ballymore ●

GALWAY

Ballinasloe

Athenry

Athlone
June 1691
taken

Galway ●

✕
Aughrim

KING'S COUNTY

Dublin
May–July 1689
James II holds
'Patriot parliament'

KILDARE

Banagher ●

L e i n s t e r

QUEEN'S COUNTY

Kilcullen

CLARE

WICKLOW

St Ruth arrives with
reinforcements for
Catholic forces
May 1691

Carlow

CARLOW

KILKENNY

CARLOW

Limerick ●
besieged
August 1690
unsuccessfully besieged
Sept.–Oct. 1691
town captured

Caherconlish ●

TIPPERARY

Kilkenny

Bennetsbridge ●

WEXFORD

LIMERICK

M u n s t e r

KERRY

Carrick-on-Suir ●

● Waterford

● Wexford

WATERFORD

CORK

Cork ● besieged and
Sept. 1690
captured

Kinsale ●
March 1689
James II lands
October 1690
besieged and
captured

3280	500
1320	400
990	300
660	200
330	100
0 ft	0 m

N

0   20 km

0   20 miles

PART IV: FROM SPLENDOUR TO FAMINE

James Kelly

COMPARED WITH the 16th and 17th centuries, the 18th century in Ireland appears quiescent and uneventful. There was, it is true, no outbreak of serious religico-political conflict until the 1790s, but both Irish society and politics were less consensual and politics more eventful than the visible absence of civil discord suggests. There is some disagreement between historians as to how we can best interpret Irish society during this period. In his provocative study of 'the making of Protestant Ireland', Sean Connolly has shown how comparable 18th-century Ireland was to other ancien régime societies. From this perspective, the tensions and conflicts that can be identified arose out of the essentially hierarchical character of its social organization, and mirror equivalent phenomena in Britain and on the continent. If this was all, it would be possible to dispense with the traditional perception that the most formative influence on Irish politics during the Georgian era was its colonial subordination to Britain and that the most consequential feature of Irish society was that the preeminently Catholic Gaelic population was ruled by an introduced Anglophone landowning élite, but the two views need not be mutually exclusive. Indeed, Irish history during this period makes more sense if both are appealed to.

Below: In all its glittering finery, a state ball held in Dublin Castle, painted by William van der Hagen in 1731.

There is certainly much to sustain a colonial interpretation from a political perspective. It is significant, for example, that the head of the Irish administration
(the Lord Lieutenant) was appointed by the Crown on the recommendation of
the British government, and was seldom entrusted to anybody other than
Englishmen. This led to the practice for much of the 18th century of lords lieutenant not residing permanently in Ireland for the duration of their posting but,
significantly, did not result in a dramatic transfer of power to Irish-born officials. Indeed, successive governments insured against this by determining that
the most important offices of state were filled by Englishmen.

Allied with this, the Crown could avail of Poynings' Law (1494), which gave
the English (from 1707, the British) Privy Council the power to respite and to
amend all legislation emanating from the Irish parliament, and to the
Declaratory Act (1719), which made the House of Lords at Westminster the
final court of legal appeal in Irish law cases and gave the British parliament the
power to make law for Ireland.

If this combination of practices and powers suggest that Ireland's position
within the British empire was irrevocably colonial, the emergence of a persua-
sive Irish Protestant critique of the dependent position to which their kingdom
was consigned, defined influentially by J. G. Simms as *colonial nationalism*,

Below: *The Dublin Volunteers
saluting the Statue of William III on
College Green, 4 November 1779.*

would seem to indicate that this was how Irish Protestants saw it as well. In fact Simms' '*colonial nationalism*' can be interpreted equally plausibly as an Irish manifestation of the Europeanwide phenomenon of civic humanism or 'patriotism' because, like its European parallels, the Irish phenomenon placed similar emphasis on political virtue and domestic economic improvement.

More significantly, from the moment it was given political coherency by William Molyneux in his seminal tract *The case of Ireland's being Bound by Acts of Parliament in England Stated* in the late 1690s, equality with Britain was the political *raison d'être* of Irish Protestant Patriots. This is why Molyneux could describe a legislative union as 'an happiness we can hardly hope for', and why the Irish parliament responded to the Anglo-Scottish union of 1707 by appealing to Queen Anne to expedite a similar arrangement with respect to Ireland. However, because neither Queen Anne nor her ministers who, like most English politicians and opinion makers, regarded and treated Ireland as a colony, could perceive any advantage in such an arrangement as long as the Irish parliament continued to vote the revenue needed to fund the Irish army establishment and to pay for the administration of the kingdom, the address was ignored.

This did not please Irish Protestants, and they responded to this and to other manifestations of British unwillingness to acknowledge their equal status under the Crown by asserting their right to govern themselves on the same terms as Englishmen and the equality of the kingdom of Ireland with that of Britain. This is why when, after many decades of pursuing this cause, the Patriots were able to take advantage of the government's difficulties in the American colonies to compel them to repeal the bulk of the laws confining Ireland's freedom to trade in 1779–80 and to accede to the removal or modification of the restrictions on the legislative authority of the Irish parliament, they did not seek to emulate the Americans and achieve independence. Quite the contrary; they did not want separation, just the power to govern. Indeed, so strong was their fear of doing anything that would endanger the Anglo-Irish connection, upon which they realized the security of their ascendant position in Ireland rested, that they made no attempt to challenge the British government's right to nominate the head of the Irish administration and declined an opportunity to reform the Irish legislature to make it more representative of the Protestant population at large.

As this, and the decision of the Irish parliament in 1800 to vote itself out of existence bears witness, a large percentage (probably a majority during the bulk of this era) of Irish Protestants preferred the security of a close (and, if necessary, a dependent) relationship with Britain, because fundamentally the maintenance of what they then termed their ascendancy *vis à vis* the Catholic population was their priority and they perceived its perpetuation as dependent upon the retention of an intimate Anglo-Irish nexus. This is why it is not a coincidence that the decade which saw the advancement by the United Irishmen of the virtues of a republic culminated with the decision of the Irish ruling élite to opt

to govern Ireland from Westminster rather than to continue to do so from College Green.

If this conforms to a colonial pattern, there is also much to sustain Connolly's view that Ireland was an *ancien régime* society. Thus, like most European countries, land was owned by a relatively small number of large landowners and worked by tenant occupiers, who were expected to defer to their social superiors and to assent to their social, economic and political dominance locally as well as nationally. Moreover, as was the case elsewhere, the members of this landed élite were convinced that they were the natural repository of government on the island because only they were equipped economically and intellectually to rule.

The situation in Ireland was complicated by the fact that the religion of the bulk of this élite (the Church of Ireland) differed from that of the majority of the population, but the élite secured itself in this respect by defining itself as the political nation and by implementing a corps of discriminatory legislation (the Penal Laws) which secured them economically, socially and politically against the Catholic majority. For most of the 18th century, indeed, their rule was unchallenged, and the fact that the Irish economy embarked on one of its most sustained periods of growth once it had negotiated poor harvests, famine and

Above: Ireland's ruling élite aristocracy and country landowners embraced the 'Georgian' style with enthusiasm. Many great houses were built or rebuilt. Shown here is Caledon, seat of the Earl of Caledon, Co.Tyrone, completed in 1794.

epidemic disease between 1725 and 1745 seemed to suggest it was advantageous to the country.

The economic, and consequent demographic expansion that was a feature of the second half of the 18th century was not due simply to the guidance of the Protestant élite. But the enthusiasm for improvement manifested by its members, the contributions they made to the success of the linen industry and to advances in internal navigation, to urban development, the enhancement of the road network, land enclosure, demesne development and 'big house' construction all attest to its weighty imprint.

This activity and the rise in population from *c.* 2 million in 1750 to *c.* 4.5 million in 1790 were the most tangible manifestations of the greater prosperity of the Irish economy, but they did not prove equally beneficial to all. Many outside the élite were gravely discommoded by the commercial forces that were released, and this led to a marked upsurge in agrarian unrest from the 1760s. This was essentially conservative in thrust for several decades, but sectarian passions lay just beneath the surface, and when they fused with the reformist and revolutionary doctrines emanating from Britain and France in the 1790s, they facilitated the dissemination of republican ideas, which in the second half of the 1790s posed the confessional *ancien regime* state and colonial Anglo-Irish nexus a formidable challenge that climaxed with the explicitly separatist intent of those who rose in rebellion in 1798.

This was overcome, but the price the Anglo-Irish élite had to pay was high because the Act of Union which followed changed the context within which Irish politics were conducted. If most Irish Protestants had no difficulty accepting this, many Catholics too were content. They believed the abolition of the Irish parliament would pave the way for the repeal of the last major penal disability—the prohibition on Catholics sitting in parliament. However, the united parliament proved less than accommodating.

As a consequence, a more broad-based and assertive Catholic leadership, spearheaded by Daniel O'Connell's Catholic Association, emerged in the 1820s to advance the issue. They eventually obliged ministers to give way in the course of which they shattered the *ancien regime* mould forever. Schooled in

the emerging precepts of democracy by the Association, O'Connell subsequently took up the repeal of the Act of Union in a vain attempt to restore domestic government to Ireland. He was unable to make much progress on the matter, but having transformed Irish politics by creating an active Catholic political interest, he also gave parliamentary politics the key feature of its political agenda for the rest of the century.

At the same time, the priority of the Catholic masses was fixed on the more elemental matter of survival. Following the ending of the Napoleonic wars, the Irish economy embarked on a period of uncertainty. Agricultural exports grew, but the economy was unable to offer security against famine to the rising number of poor and vulnerable among a population which neared 7 million in 1821. Industrialization would have reduced their vulnerability, but the failure of the cotton industry and the mechanization of linen manufacture indicated its limited potential, so that when the country's main staple foodstuff—the potato—was seriously damaged in the late 1840s, a crisis of cataclysmic proportions ensued which changed both Irish society and politics irrevocably.

Below: Lord Grandison, a landowner concerned with improving his estates, created a carefully designed housing on his estates. Below is an illustration showing a range of houses to be assigned to tradesmen on his Waterford property.

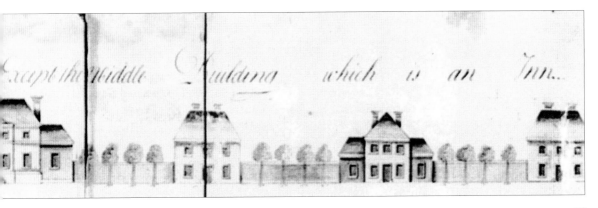

The Penal Laws

As a consequence of the military triumph of the Williamites in 1690–91, political authority in Ireland was restored to the Protestant interest, from whom it had been removed during the reign of James II. Convinced by their experiences, and their cultivation of an exaggeratedly baleful memory of the 1641 'massacres', that the Catholics were irrevocably committed to their destruction, many Protestants shared the conclusion of Edward Wetenhall, Church of Ireland bishop of Limerick, that in time there would be a repeat of the events of the 1640s and 1680s if immediate steps were not taken to weaken the Catholic interest. Such conclusions were encouraged by reports in the 1690s that Irish Catholic emigrés were actively pursuing schemes to bring about another French invasion, and by the visible Jacobitism of Catholic priests and ecclesiastics. Indeed, Wetenhall and those of like mind believed that the ratification and enforcement of anti-Catholic law was a matter not of vengeance but of survival.

Percentage of households Catholic – 1732	
Leinster	79%
Ulster	38%
Munster	89%
Connacht	91%
Nationally	73%

Anti-Catholic legislation would serve both to secure the political, economic and social ascendancy of Protestants in Ireland and to increase their number by inducing Catholics to embrace the Protestant religion. Many influential figures in the corridors of power were not convinced of the wisdom of such a course. They sought to honour the spirit of the Treaty of Limerick which offered Catholics an ambiguous promise of toleration, and ensured that no specifically anti-Catholic legislation of Irish origin was ratified in the early 1690s. However, Catholics were precluded by the adoption in 1692 of an English oath from sitting in parliament, and as Dublin Castle struggled in the mid-1690s to win the support of sufficient MPs to ensure the smooth administration of the country, they were obliged to bow to demands for laws to restrict the freedoms of Catholics and the Catholic Church. Thus in 1697, the first of a number of measures, culminating in the 1703 act for registering clergy, was ratified with the purpose of depriving Catholics of ecclesiastical leadership and of limiting the number of clergy in the country. In the years that followed, restrictions were also imposed on the freedom of Catholics to educate their children, to carry arms, inherit, own, lease and work land, to trade and employ, to enter the major professions and, finally in 1728, to vote.

Having already suffered the loss of their lands and traditional leaders to war and to emigration, the Catholics were ill-prepared to resist this legislation. The Penal Laws, as they became known, were not devised systematically to weaken Catholics in every area of life, but they did serve to exclude them from the political process until the 1790s and to hinder their economic advancement.

The Penal Laws were less effective in the religious sphere. The restrictions imposed on the Catholic Church caused serious problems nationally for a number of decades, particularly at times of Jacobite activity, and provided antipathetic landlords with plenty of opportunities to obstruct its mission. But the Church never experienced the shortage of priests or the virulent repression it endured in the early 1650s, and from the mid-1720s it enjoyed a sufficiency of clergy and the freedom to operate competently, if not without difficulty or fear.

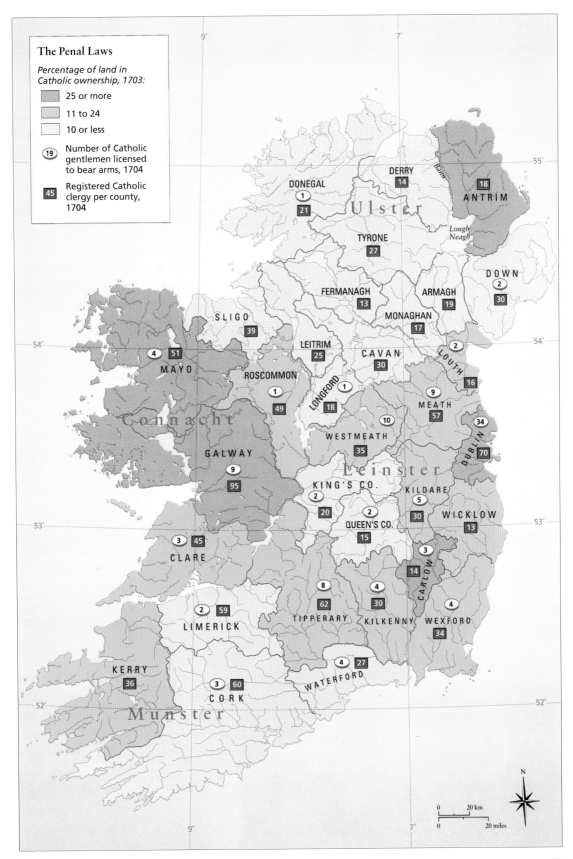

The Penal Laws

Percentage of land in Catholic ownership, 1703:

- 25 or more
- 11 to 24
- 10 or less

⑲ Number of Catholic gentlemen licensed to bear arms, 1704

45 Registered Catholic clergy per county, 1704

DONEGAL ① 21

DERRY 14

ANTRIM 18

Ulster

TYRONE 27

Lough Neagh

DOWN ② 30

FERMANAGH 13

ARMAGH 19

MONAGHAN 17

SLIGO 39

LEITRIM 25

CAVAN 30

LOUTH ② 16

MAYO ④ 51

ROSCOMMON ① 49

LONGFORD 18

LONGFORD ①

MEATH ⑨ 57

DUBLIN ㉞ ⑩ 70

Connacht

WESTMEATH ⑩ 35

Leinster

GALWAY ⑨ 95

KING'S CO. ② 20

KILDARE ⑤ 30

WICKLOW 13

QUEEN'S CO. ② 15

CLARE ③ 45

CARLOW 14 ③

LIMERICK ② 59

TIPPERARY ⑧ 62

KILKENNY ④ 30

WEXFORD ④ 34

KERRY 36

WATERFORD ④ 27

CORK ③ 60

Munster

N

0   20 km
0   20 miles

The Georgian Economy

THE INFLUENCE of the Protestant interest in Ireland peaked in the 18th century. Politically, this can be pinpointed to the 65 years between 1728 and 1793 when, as well as their exclusion from parliament, Catholics did not possess the franchise. These are the decades commonly regarded as the high-point of Protestant ascendancy, though this term is problematic because of its use by conservative Protestants from the 1780s to justify their undiluted predominance. There was a widespread Protestant perception, articulated in 1781 by Henry Flood, that they were 'the people of Ireland', an exclusive vision, but one softened by their commitment to the island's economic development. This enthusiasm for improvement took many forms, one of the most important of which was the establishment in 1711 of the Linen Board. This body enforced quality controls on the production and sale of exported linens, establishing the industry as the country's leading currency-earner and resulting in the emergence of Ulster as its wealthiest and most populous province.

Efforts by landowners to establish linen operations elsewhere in the country proved less successful, but other initiatives continued. Indeed, at both local and national levels the ruling élite assiduously sought to remould both the rural and urban landscapes in the anglican image they held dear. Some of their schemes, like the proliferation of palladian and neo-classical residences and carefully landscaped demesnes, were primarily self-serving, but they did facilitate the dissemination of new techniques in construction and internal design and employed craftsmen from a multiplicity of trades. Other improvements such as the creation of a road network, widely regarded in the late 18th century as one of the best in Europe, the enhancement of internal navigation through the construction of canals and the drainage of rivers, and the creation of a network of estate villages were less personally motivated, though they well fitted the vision of a tidy landscape. Urban development on a substantial scale was fostered in cities like Dublin, Limerick, Cork and Waterford. In Dublin the crowded warrens of medieval streets were swept away by the Wide Streets Commissioners, and a lattice of straight, broad thoroughfares linking the elegant Georgian streets and squares on the north and south sides of the River Liffey was put in their place. Combined with fine new public buildings including a new parliament, customs house, city exchange and courts, they transformed the city into one of the most attractive of the period, and a crowning symbol of the vision and achievement of the Protestant interest in Ireland.

Below: Medieval buildings were swept aside to make room for Georgian ideas of elegance in buildings and landscapes. Here the home of the Duke of Abercorn sits in its well-groomed 'landscape'.

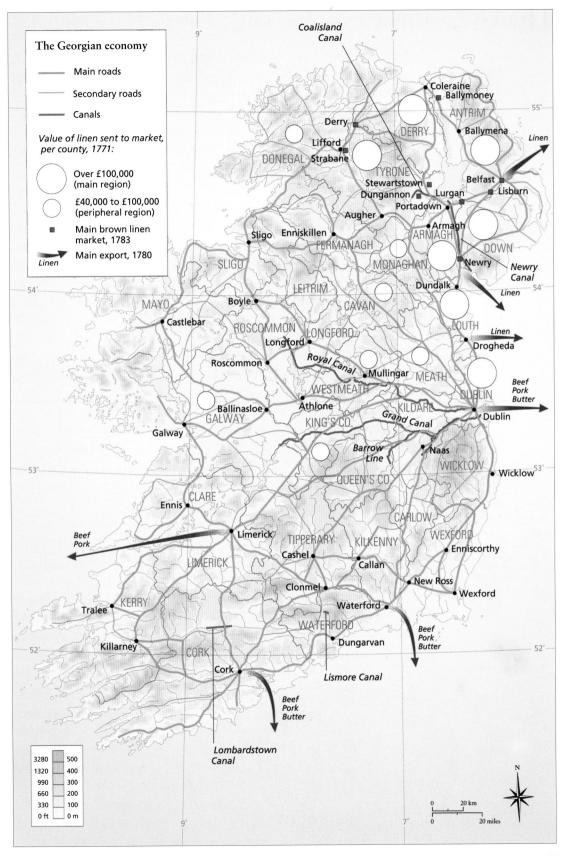

The Georgian economy

Main roads

Secondary roads

Canals

Value of linen sent to market, per county, 1771:

Over £100,000 (main region)

£40,000 to £100,000 (peripheral region)

Main brown linen market, 1783

Main export, 1780

Coalisland Canal

Coleraine
Ballymoney
ANTRIM
Derry
Lifford
Strabane
DERRY
DONEGAL
Ballymena
Linen
TYRONE
Stewartstown
Dungannon
Augher
Portadown
Belfast
Lurgan
Lisburn
Armagh
DOWN
Sligo
Enniskillen
FERMANAGH
ARMAGH
Newry
SLIGO
MONAGHAN
Newry Canal
Linen
LEITRIM
Dundalk
MAYO
Boyle
CAVAN
LONGFORD
LOUTH
Castlebar
ROSCOMMON
Longford
Linen
Roscommon
Royal Canal
Drogheda
Mullingar
MEATH
WESTMEATH
Athlone
Ballinasloe
KING'S CO.
Grand Canal
Dublin
Beef
Pork
Butter
GALWAY
Galway
Barrow Line
Naas
Dublin
WICKLOW
Wicklow
QUEEN'S CO.
CLARE
CARLOW
Ennis
WEXFORD
Beef
Pork
Limerick
TIPPERARY
KILKENNY
Enniscorthy
Cashel
Callan
KERRY
Clonmel
New Ross
Wexford
Tralee
Waterford
Beef
Pork
Butter
Killarney
CORK
WATERFORD
Dungarvan
Cork
Lismore Canal
Beef
Pork
Butter
Lombardstown
Canal

3280	500
1320	400
990	300
660	200
330	100
0 ft	0 m

N

0   20 km

0   20 miles

The Government of Ireland, 1692–1785

LONDON'S decision in the early 1690s to entrust the responsibility of raising revenue and making law to an Irish parliament determined the character of 18th-century government. Like its British counterpart, the Irish parliament had two chambers. The House of Lords consisted of a fluctuating number of temporal and a fixed number of religious peers, while the House of Commons comprised 300 representatives chosen from 150 constituencies of varying antiquity and franchise. It was an exclusively Protestant assembly because of the Irish parliament's decision to follow the Westminster precedent requiring all members to swear an oath of adjuration. The parliament sat for approximately six months every two years between 1692 and 1784, and annually thereafter, affording Irish Protestants a central role in the administration of their kingdom. The parliament's powers, however, were severely circumscribed by Poynings' Law and the Declaratory Act, and by the fact that the Irish executive at Dublin Castle was not responsible to parliament and that its head, the Lord Lieutenant, was a nominee of the British government.

Despite these constraints, the members of the Irish parliament, particularly the Commons, sought to play an active part in the administration of the kingdom. Because of this, and the disinclination of successive lords lieutenant to keep tight personal control of the levers of power by residing in Ireland throughout the terms of their appointment, the day-to-day duties of administration were shared between English-born officeholders and able Irish politicians (commonly termed undertakers) who agreed, in return for preferment and influence, to manage the parliament on the Lord Lieutenant's behalf.

This arrangement worked satisfactorily from its inception in 1695 until the 1750s, when a disruptive power struggle between Henry Boyle and John Ponsonby prompted a reassessment, and it was decided, eventually, that lords lieutenant should reside in Ireland for the duration of their appointment.

The decision of Lord Townshend to become a residential lord lieutenant in the late 1760s contributed to the emergence of the 'Patriots', whose object was to dilute the legal constraints on the legislative authority of the Irish parliament and to secure the right to free trade. Detachments of Volunteers —loosely organized associations of armed men whose primary purpose was to support the regular army— became politicized, and their extra-parliamentary lobbying was decisive in securing both free trade (1780) and legislative independence (1782). However, their attempts to secure direct admission to the political process by reforming the electoral system were thwarted by the small and unrepresentative élite that controlled most of the parliamentary constituencies.

Above: Silver-gilt mace, the symbol of authority of the old Irish House of Lords. This elegant silver work was made in Dublin around 1760.

Left: This medallion was presented to the 1st Ulster Regiment of Irish Volunteers and would be worn by the best shot in the regiment 'so long as he shall maintain his superior skill at the target'.

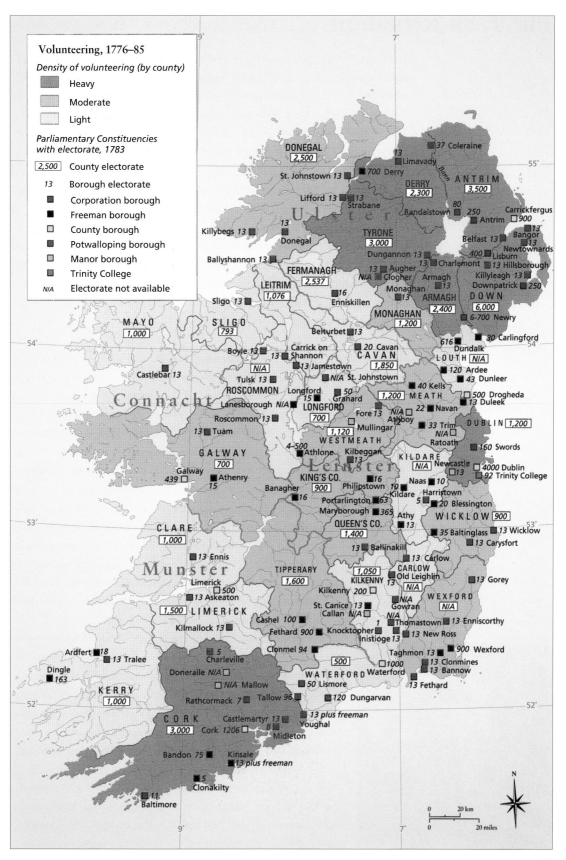

Volunteering, 1776–85

Density of volunteering (by county)

▨	Heavy
▨	Moderate
▢	Light

Parliamentary Constituencies with electorate, 1783

2,500	County electorate
13	Borough electorate
◼	Corporation borough
◼	Freeman borough
◻	County borough
◼	Potwalloping borough
◻	Manor borough
◼	Trinity College
N/A	Electorate not available

The 1798 Rebellion

THOUGH THE impression is often given, it is not true to say that 18th-century Ireland was peaceful until its last decade. The readiness of rural protesters to swathe themselves in Jacobite white suggests that they were already politicized, and that ancient sectarian loyalties remained strong. This conclusion is reinforced by the emergence in County Armagh in the 1780s of the Catholic Defenders to resist disarming raids by Protestant Peep O'Day Boys. At the same time, elements within the Protestant and Presbyterian middle classes offered an alternative non-sectarian vision and they were encouraged by the outbreak of the French Revolution in 1789 to launch a campaign to reform the representative system to satisfy their wishes. The organization they established in 1791 to spearhead their campaign took the name United Irishmen from Wolfe Tone's inspirational claim that it would only be possible to overcome the country's problems if Catholic, Protestant and Dissenter came together and Ireland broke the connection with England.

To begin with, the United Irishmen devoted their energies to the cause of reforming the representative system. Catholics were indeed conceded the franchise in 1793, but the fact that it was implemented on the insistence of London indicates how unimportant were the United Irishmen's efforts. The conservative dominated parliament embarked at the same time on a strategy to weaken its radical critics by replacing the Volunteers with a Castle-controlled militia. However, instead of destroying the movement, this strategy allowed revolutionary separatists within the organization to capitalize on the growing discontent throughout the country with the government's uncompromising policies and the premature recall, in 1795, of the liberal Lord Lieutenant, Earl Fitzwilliam. The United Irishmen then formed an alliance with the Catholic Defenders, and the movement was reconstituted along revolutionary lines. They were remarkably successful in recruiting members and in disseminating their message and, encouraged by the success of Wolfe Tone's diplomatic efforts to enlist the support of the French, were hopeful that a successful rebellion could be orchestrated.

Below: *Members of the Society of United Irishmen take an oath to rise against English rule.*

A large-scale invasion force attempted to land off Bantry Bay in 1796; if the fleet had not been disrupted by bad weather, the United Irishmen might have had a chance. Instead, the authorities were given time to embark on a ruthless campaign of disarmament. The damage inflicted on the organization ensured that when rebellion broke out in May 1798 it was fragmented and localized, being confined for the most part to east Ulster and, especially, County Wexford. Some French support was dispatched, but it came too late to alter the outcome, and the Crown forces won the day. The political initiative remained firmly in the hands of the establishment and the 1790s concluded, not with the declaration of the republic sought by the radicals, but with a legislative union.

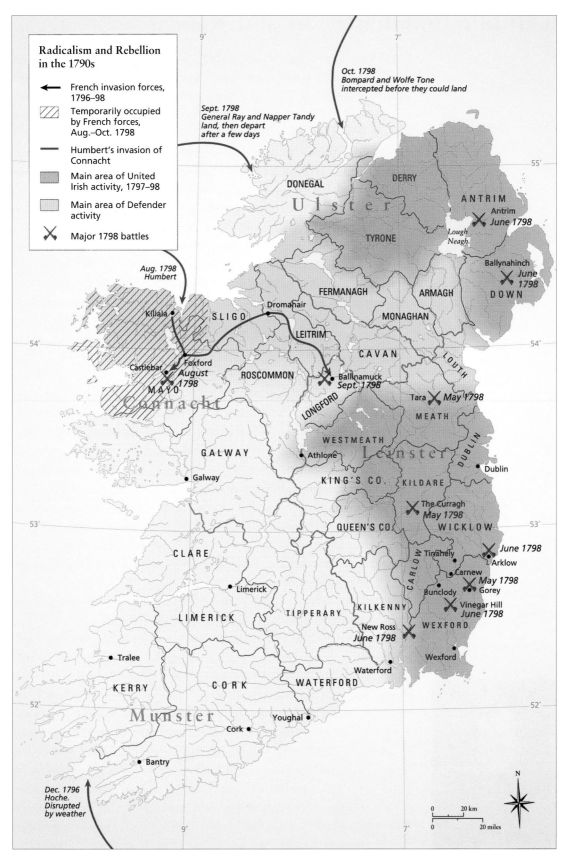

Radicalism and Rebellion in the 1790s

← French invasion forces, 1796–98

▨ Temporarily occupied by French forces, Aug.–Oct. 1798

— Humbert's invasion of Connacht

▓ Main area of United Irish activity, 1797–98

░ Main area of Defender activity

✕ Major 1798 battles

Oct. 1798
Bompard and Wolfe Tone intercepted before they could land

Sept. 1798
General Ray and Napper Tandy land, then depart after a few days

Aug. 1798
Humbert

Dec. 1796
Hoche.
Disrupted
by weather

Ulster

DONEGAL
DERRY
ANTRIM
Antrim June 1798
Lough Neagh
TYRONE
Ballynahinch June 1798
DOWN
FERMANAGH
ARMAGH
MONAGHAN
Killala
SLIGO
Dromahair
LEITRIM
CAVAN
LOUTH
Castlebar
Foxford August 1798
MAYO
Connacht
ROSCOMMON
Ballinamuck Sept. 1798
LONGFORD
Tara May 1798
MEATH
WESTMEATH
Leinster
Athlone
GALWAY
DUBLIN
Galway
KING'S CO.
KILDARE
Dublin
The Curragh May 1798
WICKLOW
CLARE
QUEEN'S CO.
June 1798
Tinahely
Arklow
Limerick
Carnew
CARLOW
May 1798
Bunclody
Gorey
KILKENNY
Vinegar Hill June 1798
LIMERICK
TIPPERARY
WEXFORD
New Ross June 1798
Tralee
Wexford
KERRY
CORK
WATERFORD
Waterford
Munster
Youghal
Cork
Bantry

N

0   20 km
0   20 miles

83

Catholic Emancipation and Repeal

FOLLOWING the repeal between 1778 and 1792 of the bulk of the laws restricting the liberty of Catholics to worship, to own and lease land, to educate their children and to enter the professions, and the enfranchisement in 1793 of Catholic 40-shilling freeholders, the major remaining infraction of Catholic civil rights was the prohibition on their sitting in parliament. Hopes were raised in 1794–95 and in 1799–1800 that Catholic emancipation would not be long delayed, but Protestant conservatives in both kingdoms remained firmly opposed. In 1801, William Pitt failed to overcome royal opposition and was unable to honour an assurance he had given Catholics during the union negotiations. Together Catholics and Whig sympathizers like Henry Grattan tried to overcome Protestant resistance by proposing a Crown 'veto' over ecclesiastical appointments, but this only helped to fragment the pro-emancipation lobby. For many Catholics, including the bishops, the proposed veto powers went too far, and Daniel O'Connell emerged as the leader of those Catholics who chose to endure exclusion rather than to accept conditional emancipation.

By the early 1820s, O'Connell had concluded that a new strategy was necessary and, following the foundation of the Catholic Association in 1823, he oversaw its transformation into one of the most remarkable agencies of popular politicization yet seen in Ireland or Europe. As a consequence, in the landmark general election of 1826, Catholics throughout the country cast off the bonds of deference and returned MPs sympathetic to their cause. Catholic confidence was further boosted two years later when O'Connell won a remarkable by-election victory in County Clare, and fearful that the resultant rise in sectarian animosity could precipitate serious civil discord, the duke of Wellington persuaded the reluctant George IV to concede to Catholics the right to sit in parliament.

Emboldened by this, in 1830 O'Connell launched a campaign to repeal the Act of Union. The campaign did not register the decisive impression he hoped for, but it provided him with an issue around which he could organize an Irish party at Westminster. On the back of some striking electoral successes in the early and mid-1830s, O'Connell forged a working alliance with the Whigs to secure a number of adminstrative and political reforms. However, following the return of the Tories to power in 1841, he devoted his energies to repeal. Supported by an energetic group of intellectual nationalists called the Young Irelanders, by the Church and by his own formidable Repeal Association, O'Connell organized a series of 'monster meetings' in 1843 with the object of compelling the government to concede Ireland 'full and prompt justice or repeal'. Ministers, however, were unyielding, and following the proscription of the meeting scheduled for Clontarf in October and O'Connell's subsequent imprisonment, he spent his final years vainly trying to retrieve lost ground.

Below: Daniel O'Connell, known as 'The Liberator', was one of the most charismatic leaders of his generation and enjoyed a reputation as a libertarian that extended far beyond Ireland's shores.

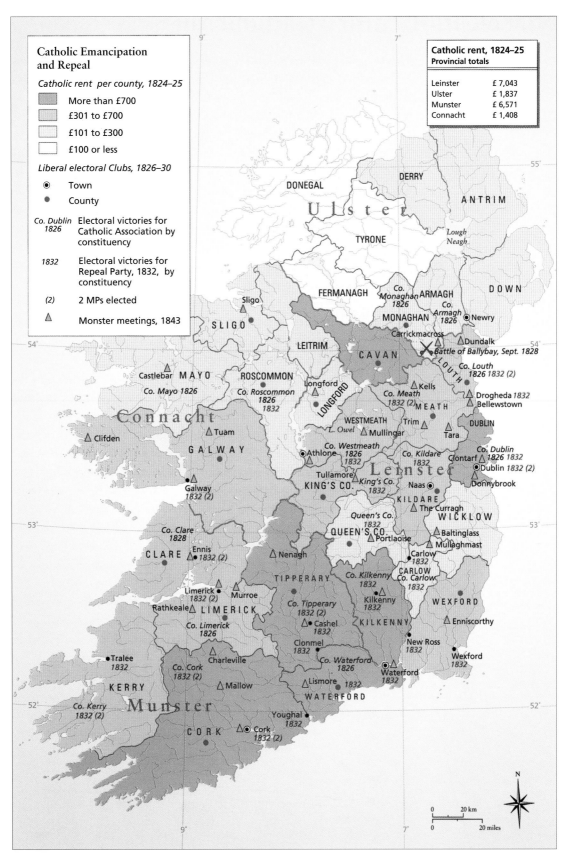

Catholic Emancipation and Repeal

Catholic rent per county, 1824–25

- More than £700
- £301 to £700
- £101 to £300
- £100 or less

Liberal electoral Clubs, 1826–30

- ◉ Town
- ● County

Co. Dublin 1826 — Electoral victories for Catholic Association by constituency

1832 — Electoral victories for Repeal Party, 1832, by constituency

(2) — 2 MPs elected

△ — Monster meetings, 1843

Catholic rent, 1824–25	
Provincial totals	
Leinster	£ 7,043
Ulster	£ 1,837
Munster	£ 6,571
Connacht	£ 1,408

DONEGAL

DERRY

Ulster

ANTRIM

TYRONE

DOWN

FERMANAGH

Co. Monaghan 1826

ARMAGH

Co. Armagh 1826

Lough Neagh

MONAGHAN

◉ Newry

Sligo ●

Carrickmacross

△ Dundalk

✕ *Battle of Ballybay, Sept. 1828*

SLIGO

LEITRIM

CAVAN

LOUTH

Co. Louth 1826 1832 (2)

Castlebar △ MAYO

Co. Mayo 1826

ROSCOMMON

Co. Roscommon 1826 1832

Longford △

LONGFORD

△ Kells

Co. Meath 1832 (2)

MEATH

△ Drogheda *1832*
△ Bellewstown

Connacht

△ Tuam

WESTMEATH

Trim △

L. Owel △ Mullingar

Tara △

DUBLIN

△ Clifden

GALWAY

◉ Athlone

Co. Westmeath 1826 1832

Co. Kildare 1832

Clontarf △ *1826 1832*

◉ Dublin *1832 (2)*

Co. Dublin

△ Galway
1832 (2)

Tullamore △

KING'S CO.

King's Co. 1832

Naas ◉

△ Donnybrook

KILDARE

Queen's Co. 1832

△ The Curragh

WICKLOW

Co. Clare 1828

CLARE

Ennis ●
△ *1832 (2)*

QUEEN'S CO.

Portlaoise △

△ Nenagh

Baltinglass △

△ Mullaghmast

TIPPERARY

Co. Kilkenny 1832

Carlow ●
△ *1832*

CARLOW

Co. Carlow 1832

Limerick ●
△ *1832 (2)*

△ Murroe

Kilkenny △ *1832*

WEXFORD

Rathkeale △ LIMERICK

Co. Tipperary 1832 (2)

● Cashel *1832*

KILKENNY

△ Enniscorthy

Co. Limerick 1826

Clonmel △ *1832*

New Ross △ *1832*

● Tralee *1832*

△ Charleville

Co. Cork 1832 (2)

△ Mallow

△ Lismore *1832*

Co. Waterford 1826

◉ △ Waterford *1832*

Wexford △ *1832*

KERRY

Munster

WATERFORD

Co. Kerry 1832 (2)

Youghal △ *1832*

CORK

△ ◉ Cork *1832 (2)*

N

0 — 20 km

0 — 20 miles

Nineteenth-Century Catholicism

DESPITE THE Penal Laws, it is clear from the returns made by Catholic bishops to Dublin Castle that the Church in 1800 was better provided with priests than it had been a century earlier. It was also embarked on a campaign of church refurbishment and construction that was to see the humble thatched dwellings identified with the Penal era being replaced by the ornate, prominent stone edifices of the 19th century. The pace of this development varied from diocese to diocese, and within each diocese from parish to parish, depending on its leadership and resources. Widespread improvements commenced in the second half of the 18th century and accelerated in the early 19th, with the wealthier dioceses of Dublin and Cashel progressing more rapidly than those of Tuam and Armagh.

One important index of the growing strength of the Catholic Church is provided by the swelling ranks of its priests and nuns. In the first half of the 19th century their numbers were insufficient to permit the Church to administer equally to all its members: in 1840 there was one priest per 3,000 people. This problem was most acute in Connacht, and it is not surprising that in 1834 the Commissioners of Public Instruction found the church attendance here lower than elsewhere. In Connacht also there was the strongest adherence to popular religious practices associated with wakes, patterns and holy wells. These practices were a primary target for the burgeoning ranks of the Maynooth-trained secular clergy who oversaw the gradual countrywide extension of the Tridentine orthodoxies laid down by Reformist bishops like Murray of Dublin and Doyle of Kildare and Leighlin. Also, the Great Famine dealt its heaviest blows in the sectors of Irish society in which such practices were most deeply entrenched, and reduced the priest-people ratio in 1870 to 1:1,250. This alleviated endemic problems of clerical indiscipline and paved the way for the provision to all Catholics of a comprehensive religious service from birth to death. Indeed, priests became their communities' moral policemen, and as the Church continued to grow in wealth, numbers and influence, it assumed responsibility for an increasing network of social functions — schools, orphanages, hospitals, asylums and so on — through which it conveyed its message.

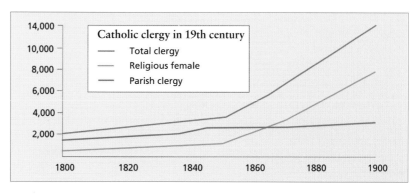

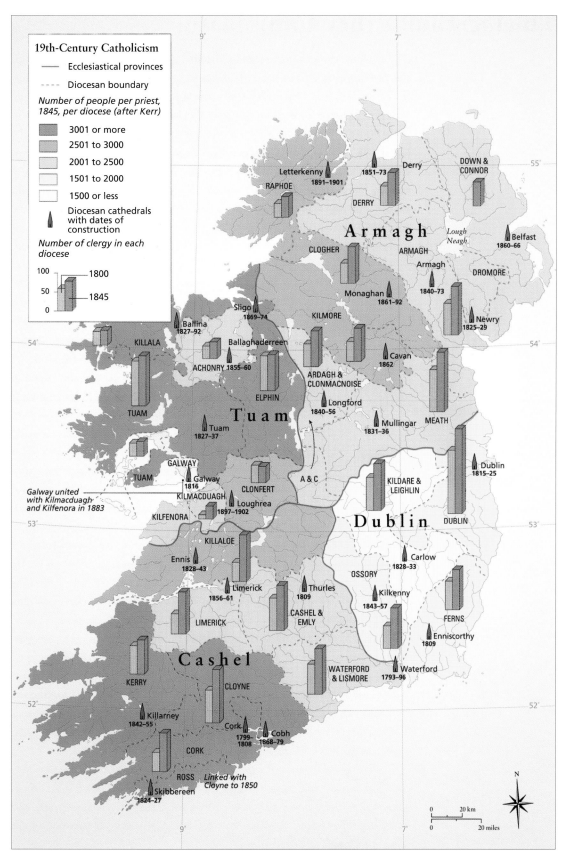

19th-Century Catholicism

— Ecclesiastical provinces

--- Diocesan boundary

Number of people per priest, 1845, per diocese (after Kerr)

3001 or more

2501 to 3000

2001 to 2500

1501 to 2000

1500 or less

Diocesan cathedrals with dates of construction

Number of clergy in each diocese

100

50

0

1800

1845

RAPHOE

Letterkenny 1891–1901

Derry 1851–73

DERRY

DOWN & CONNOR

55°

A r m a g h

CLOGHER

ARMAGH

Lough Neagh

Belfast 1860–66

Armagh 1840–73

DROMORE

Monaghan 1861–92

Newry 1825–29

Sligo 1869–74

KILMORE

Ballina 1827–92

KILLALA

Ballaghaderreen

Cavan 1862

54°

ACHONRY 1855–60

ARDAGH & CLONMACNOISE

54°

ELPHIN

MEATH

TUAM

T u a m

Tuam 1827–37

Longford 1840–56

Mullingar 1831–36

GALWAY

Galway 1816

A & C

Dublin 1815–25

KILDARE & LEIGHLIN

Galway united with Kilmacduagh and Kilfenora in 1883

TUAM

KILMACDUAGH

CLONFERT

Loughrea 1897–1902

D u b l i n

53°

KILFENORA

KILLALOE

DUBLIN

53°

Ennis 1828–43

Carlow 1828–33

OSSORY

Limerick 1856–61

Thurles 1809

Kilkenny 1843–57

FERNS

LIMERICK

CASHEL & EMLY

Enniscorthy 1809

C a s h e l

Waterford 1793–96

WATERFORD & LISMORE

KERRY

CLOYNE

52°

52°

Killarney 1842–55

Cork 1799–1808

Cobh 1868–79

CORK

ROSS *Linked with Cloyne to 1850*

Skibbereen 1824–27

N

0   20 km

0   20 miles

The Pre-Famine Economy

THE STRONG growth registered by the Irish economy in the second half of the 18th century and in the early years of the 19th came to an abrupt halt in the mid-1810s. The deflationary fiscal policy of the post-Napoleonic War government hit the banking sector especially hard, but the decline in the volume of linen and in the value of agricultural goods exported in the late 1810s indicates that the problem went deeper. The crisis was most acute in the countryside, which was affected not only by the agricultural slump, but by the general economic downturn, for much of Ireland's manufacturing was domestically based. It was compounded too by the country's demographic position: by 1820 its rising population neared 7 million.

Above: *Weighing potatoes, the staple of the agrarian community. Reliance on this single crop, together with the relative unsophistication of the Irish economy, left country people, particularly in the West, vulnerable to sudden change.*

In the late 18th century this had been accommodated by expanding employment in linen and tillage, and by the subdivision of holdings by landowners and middlemen. So long as domestic and international conditions were favourable, and the landless and landed labourers (cottiers) who constituted 56 per cent of the labour in 1841 could rely on the potato, this rising population was not a cause of concern. However, as rent arrears climbed sharply in the early 19th century, it quickly became apparent that substantial holdings were more economically viable than small tenancies. Evictions increased, but the sheer number of tenants on most estates and their mutual solidarity prevented all but the most determined landlords from restructuring land occupancy along sound economic lines. Cottiers and labourers eked out a precarious existence, but while the potato remained free from disease they remained reasonably well nourished.

In 1841 farmers with more than 50 acres represented only four per cent of the labour force. They had a ready market in industrial Britain for their grain, cattle and butter. Ulster linen-workers also found a market in Britain, but were threatened by mechanization. From the 1820s the development of machine-spinning and particularly of wet spinning forced a dramatic contraction in hand spinning in north Leinster, north Connacht and south, west and central Ulster. It appeared briefly that linen might be displaced by cotton, but the construction of a linen mill in 1828 on the site of a burnt-out Belfast cotton works indicated that the industry had a brighter future, and the building of another 60 in the north-east within a decade confirmed this.

This was the only area of Ireland to industrialize. Elsewhere, there were successful individual enterprises such as the Guinness brewery, but few successful industrial sectors. The proportion of the population engaged in trade and manufacture between 1821 and 1841 fell by 15 per cent, demonstrating the general weakness of the economy.

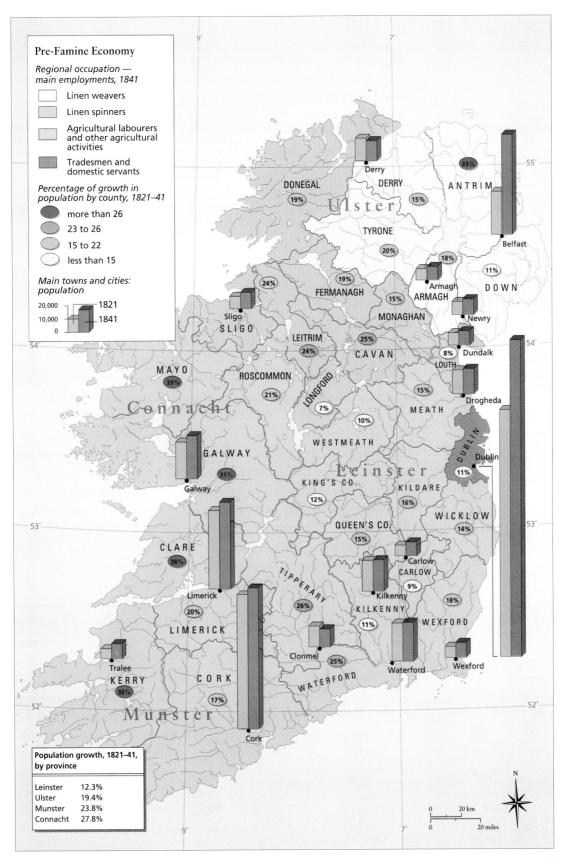

Pre-Famine Economy

Regional occupation —
main employments, 1841

- Linen weavers
- Linen spinners
- Agricultural labourers and other agricultural activities
- Tradesmen and domestic servants

Percentage of growth in population by county, 1821–41

- more than 26
- 23 to 26
- 15 to 22
- less than 15

Main towns and cities: population

20,000 · 1821
10,000 · 1841
0

DONEGAL 19%
DERRY 15%
Derry
ANTRIM 33%
Belfast
TYRONE 20%
FERMANAGH 19%
ARMAGH 18%
Armagh 15%
DOWN 11%
Newry
SLIGO 24%
Sligo
LEITRIM 24%
MONAGHAN 15%
CAVAN 25%
LOUTH 8%
Dundalk
Drogheda 15%
MAYO 33%
ROSCOMMON 21%
LONGFORD 7%
MEATH 10%
WESTMEATH
GALWAY 31%
Galway
KING'S CO. 12%
KILDARE 16%
DUBLIN
Dublin 11%
WICKLOW 14%
CLARE 38%
Limerick
QUEEN'S CO. 15%
CARLOW 9%
Carlow
Kilkenny
LIMERICK 20%
TIPPERARY 26%
KILKENNY 11%
WEXFORD 18%
Wexford
Clonmel
Tralee
KERRY 36%
CORK 17%
WATERFORD 25%
Waterford
Cork

Ulster
Connacht
Leinster
Munster

Population growth, 1821–41, by province	
Leinster	12.3%
Ulster	19.4%
Munster	23.8%
Connacht	27.8%

N

0   20 km
0   20 miles

Emigration to 1845

THOUGH THE Irish are today widely perceived as an emigrant people, emigration from the island is in fact only a comparatively recent phenomenon. Prior to the 18th century, the country gained more people than it lost.

The best known of 18th-century Irish emigration was that of the Ulster Scots, who were tempted by the opportunities in the American colonies, and chose to settle there in small numbers from the late 1710s, rising to as many as 50,000 in the early 1770s. Much of this emigration, distinct from the seasonal migrations to Britain and Newfoundland, was by relatively affluent families, but the practice of indentured servitude provided a means by which the poor and restless could also leave.

The American War of Independence (1775–83) temporarily prevented access to what had become the main destination for Irish emigrants. By the early 1770s emigration to America was an established aspect of Irish life, though it was small enough to make little impression on the fast-growing population.

From 1827, the number of emigrants to North America exceeded 20,000 for the first time since the 1780s, and the trend was upwards. In 1831–32, it reached 65,000 for the first time, and average annual emigration to North America exceeded 65,000 between 1841 and 1845. In total, almost 1 million people left Ireland for North America between 1815 and 1845, and while a majority of these first set foot on Canadian soil, this was a reflection of the cost of their passage, not their choice of destination.

While to reach the United States was the ambition of most Irish emigrants, an increasing number were also drawn to industrial Britain. There were significant concentrations of Irish in several English cities by 1800, but these were dwarfed by the 500,000 or so emigrants that moved to Britain in the early 19th century. This trend may reflect the strong tradition of seasonal migration to Britain that had been established in the 18th century.

Below: *People gather at the Government Inspector's Office determined to take a ship for America. Engraving from the Illustrated London News .*

Irish convicts were transported to Australia from the late 1780s, when America's newly-won independence ruled it out as an option. Between the 1780s and 1845, Australia was the destination of between 50,000 and 65,000 Irish felons. A minority, among them some United Irishmen, were political prisoners, but most were common criminals exiled by a penal system that preferred expulsion to the cost of imprisonment.

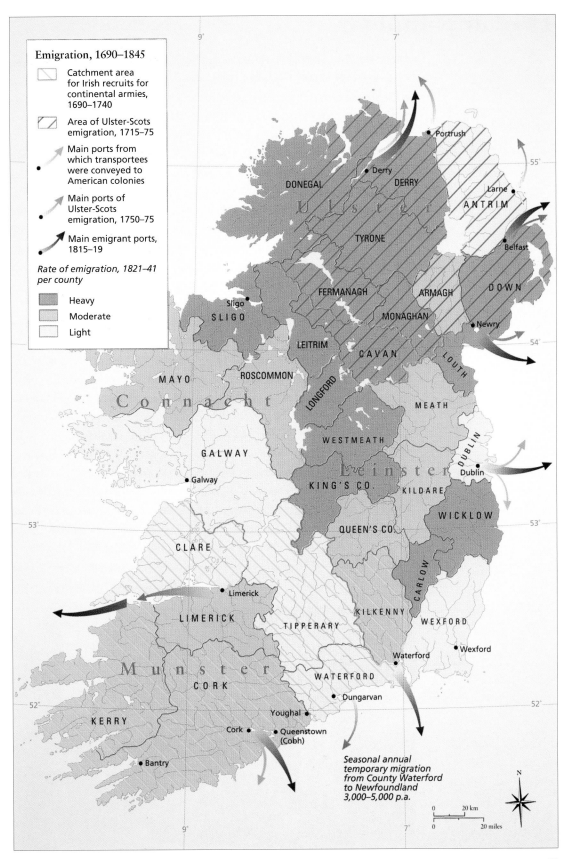

Emigration, 1690–1845

Catchment area for Irish recruits for continental armies, 1690–1740

Area of Ulster-Scots emigration, 1715–75

Main ports from which transportees were conveyed to American colonies

Main ports of Ulster-Scots emigration, 1750–75

Main emigrant ports, 1815–19

Rate of emigration, 1821–41 per county

Heavy

Moderate

Light

Seasonal annual temporary migration from County Waterford to Newfoundland 3,000–5,000 p.a.

The Great Famine

IRELAND LIVED under the threat of famine throughout the early 19th century. Between 1800 and 1845 there were some 16 food crises most of which were caused by adverse weather conditions. Because the emergencies were generally overcome with relatively modest loss of life, there was no reason to anticipate an epic disaster, and the fact that the country annually produced enough food, not just to feed its own population but to export a healthy surplus gives the lie to those who maintain that the Great Famine was a disaster waiting to happen. Population growth had already declined appreciably from its 18th-century peak, and by the early 1840s increasing numbers were emigrating. The rural poor were nevertheless vulnerable to disaster, and in 1845 it came from Europe in the form of an incurable fungal disease, Phytophthera infestans, which decimated their staple food stuff, the potato crop.

The blight spread rapidly because of the wet harvest season, and 40 per cent of the crop was destroyed. This was enough to plunge the country into crisis, though imports of Indian meal at first kept mortality within bounds. If the blight had not recurred, the setback of 1845 would not have been much more consequential than any of the previous regional crises. Unfortunately, in three of the following four years the potato blight again took a heavy toll, with the result that when relief from private and official sources proved inadequate, tens of thousands died annually from malnutrition and epidemic disease. According to recent calculations approximately 1 million people died, of which an estimated 40 per cent came from Connacht, 30 per cent from Munster, 21 per cent from Ulster and 9 per cent from Leinster. Inevitably the crisis was most severe in the poorest areas: death and emigration reduced the population to 6.5 million, with the proportion of landholdings of less than five acres falling from 35 to 20 per cent, and those of 15 or more acres rising from 31 to 48 per cent between 1841 and 1851. Post-Famine rural Ireland was to be quite different as a consequence.

Right: *The poor and destitute gather outside the gates of a workhouse hoping for shelter and food. By 1847 the local systems of relief were utterly overwhelmed by the magnitude of the crisis.*

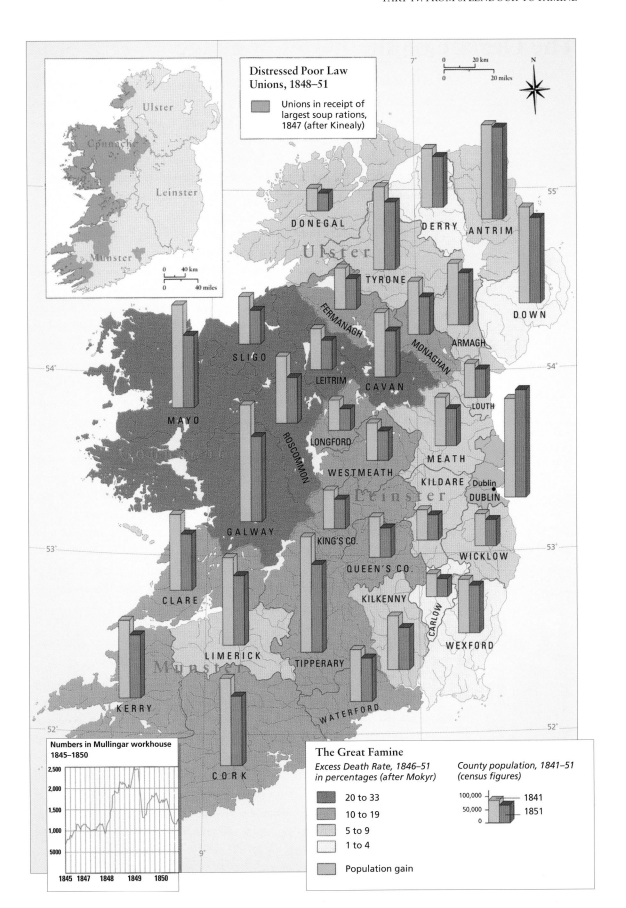

Distressed Poor Law Unions, 1848–51

Unions in receipt of largest soup rations, 1847 (after Kinealy)

0   20 km
0   20 miles

N

ULSTER

DONEGAL
DERRY
ANTRIM
TYRONE
FERMANAGH
DOWN
MONAGHAN
ARMAGH
SLIGO
LEITRIM
CAVAN
LOUTH
MAYO
LONGFORD
ROSCOMMON
MEATH
WESTMEATH
KILDARE Dublin
DUBLIN
Leinster
GALWAY
KING'S CO.
WICKLOW
CLARE
QUEEN'S CO.
KILKENNY
CARLOW
WEXFORD
LIMERICK
TIPPERARY
Munster
KERRY
WATERFORD
CORK

Connacht

0   40 km
0   40 miles

Ulster
Connacht
Leinster
Munster

Numbers in Mullingar workhouse 1845–1850

2,500
2,000
1,500
1,000
5000

1845 1847 1848 1849 1850

The Great Famine

Excess Death Rate, 1846–51 in percentages (after Mokyr)

- 20 to 33
- 10 to 19
- 5 to 9
- 1 to 4

- Population gain

County population, 1841–51 (census figures)

100,000 ──── 1841
50,000   1851
0

The Decline of the Irish Language

The Irish language, of which Scottish Gaelic and Manx are dialects, is of Celtic and ultimately Indo-European origin, and has been spoken in Ireland for perhaps 2,500 years. Although it began to exhibit some minor Norse influences in the aftermath of the Viking invasions, its position as the language of Ireland only underwent serious challenge with the introduction of substantial communities of English speakers in the aftermath of the English invasion in the late 12th century.

Nevertheless, Irish retained its dominance, and, indeed, by the 14th century was spoken by an increasing number of settlers, Gaelic culture undergoing a considerable resurgence, in spite of attempts by the Dublin government to legislate against it. English language and influence were never eradicated, however, especially from the towns, and the Tudor reconquest put Irish very much on the defensive. By the early 17th century, the native aristocracy, the principal patrons of Gaelic culture, had been overthrown, and the language lost its ascendancy. Plantation of new English-speaking settlers, and a comprehensive redistribution of landownership following the Cromwellian and Williamite wars, meant that the new proprietorial, professional and mercantile classes were English-speaking virtually without exception.

Although Gaelic literature survived, and its merits increasingly gained an antiquarian appreciation, it was now predominantly the expression of an underclass, and for those anxious to gain social or economic advancement a knowledge of English was essential. Ironically, as the population began to rise rapidly, by the early 19th century there were probably more Irish-speakers than at any time previously (4 million or more), but they were the poorest sections of society, and an accelerating abandonment of Irish had begun well before the Great Famine struck in the mid-1840s. Death and massive emigration had the effect of decimating the language, aided by a hostile education system and a largely unsympathetic Church, so that by the end of the century its future seemed bleak.

At this point, however, a vibrant language revival movement emerged in the form of the Gaelic League (*Conradh na Gaeilge*), interest growing in tandem with the demand for political independence. The establishment of the Irish Free State in 1922 had the not entirely healthy effect of institutionalizing the language movement (except in the six counties which became Northern Ireland) and government efforts to promote Irish, especially by maintaining the viability of the Gaeltacht, the remaining Irish-speaking areas, and insisting on compulsory instruction in schools, have thus far attained only limited success. Perhaps the best hope for the language's future lies in the enthusiasm which individual groups of parents are showing for the provision of all-Irish primary education for their children in the form of *Gaelscoileanna*.

Below: *Early premises of* Conradh na Gaeilge *(the Gaelic League) in Sackville Street, around the turn of the century.*

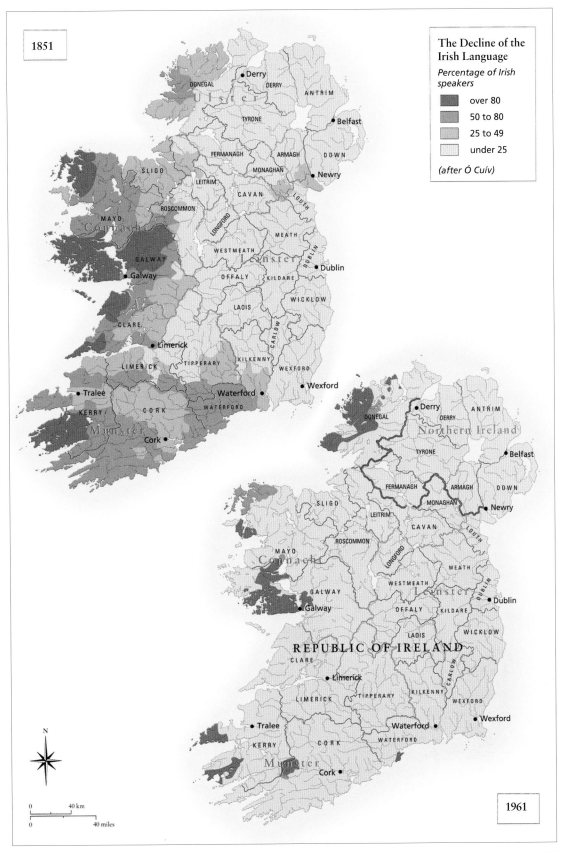

1851

The Decline of the Irish Language
Percentage of Irish speakers

- over 80
- 50 to 80
- 25 to 49
- under 25

(after Ó Cuív)

1961

Part V: Modern Ireland

Gabriel Doherty

AT FIRST SIGHT the history of Ireland over the course of the last 150 years manifests many similarities with the process of political, economic and social modernization evident in the evolution of its western European neighbours during the same period. A market-oriented economy characterized by a commercialized agricultural sector and substantially augmented manufacturing and service sectors; a literate population, increasingly urbanized, who live longer, marry less and have smaller families compared to their forebears; a sophisticated social welfare system designed to cater for the multifarious needs of its citizens; and a social culture which has become daily more variegated and influenced by international trends — in all these respects and more Ireland has changed since the Famine and changed quite dramatically, but only, it appears, to become less distinctively national and more routinely cosmopolitan.

Below: Charles Stewart Parnell entered parliament in 1875 and was active in the 'obstructionist' faction of the Home Rule Party. Their intention was to obstruct the day-to-day business of parliament in order to highlight Irish issues.

Other important changes should also be noted, most notably the dramatic decline in the island's population since the Famine (which stands in stark contrast to the unprecedented rate of expansion in the pre-Famine era, and also to the expansion evident elsewhere in Europe since the middle of the last century) and the formal partition of the island in 1920 into two distinct political entities. This latter development in particular, although in some respects only the formal political confirmation of a pattern of regional social and economic differentiation evident for over a century, nonetheless marked a significant point of departure for the subsequent history of the island, albeit not a very propitious one.

Such changes notwithstanding, however, there are characteristics of Irish life which have withstood the passage of time and which continue to set off Irish politics and society from those obtaining in other countries. The issues of ownership, dis-

Below: *Presidents John F. Kennedy and Éamon de Valera together during JFK's triumphant visit to Ireland in June 1963. He was seen as the supreme symbol of Irish-American success and was received like a conquering hero. But he had barely four month to live.*

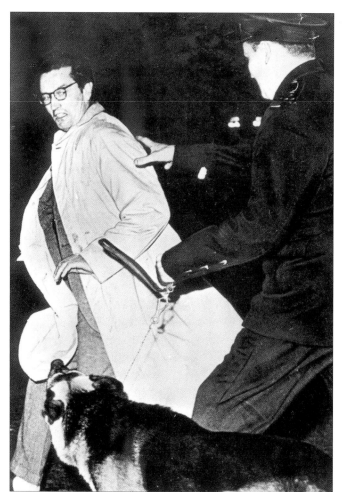

Below: Dr Noel Browne, seen here being chased by police following a protest outside the American embassy in Dublin in the 1960s, had been Minister for Health from 1948 to 1951. A passionate socialist and radical, he had spearheaded the campaign which effectively eradicated tuberculosis as an epidemic disease in Ireland. In doing so, he removed one of the country's greatest scourges.

tribution and utilization of land have proved to be as contentious in this era as they were in the more distant past. The 'quiet revolution', by which ownership of land was transferred in the late 19th and early 20th centuries from landlord to tenant, was effected with less difficulty than many expected bearing in mind its uniquely controversial history, but changes in formal patterns of tenure were less significant than the contemporaneous and accelerated shift from arable to pastoral usage. While similar developments were taking place elsewhere, the social consequences of such a reorientation were perhaps more problematic for Ireland than for any other western European country, given the complex political context within which it took place, although one should note that the political disturbances of the period between 1915 and 1923 were not, in the main, economically determined.

Concern with land, however, has not been the only issue which has served to highlight the continuities between the pre- and post-Famine eras. The enduring cultural achievements of the Irish people, exemplified in the international acclaim accorded to such outstanding literary figures as Oscar Wilde, George Bernard Shaw, W.B. Yeats, James Joyce, Samuel Beckett and, more recently, Seamus Heaney, have also been widely attested to. Less straightforward has been the intellectual legacy of modern Irish nationalism which has provided the inspiration for some of the most dramatic developments of the period, most obviously the achievement of political independence for the greater part of the island under the terms of the 1921 Anglo-Irish Treaty, but which, in common with the equally problematic phenomenon of unionism, has left a complex and frequently divisive mark on the political and social landscape of the north-eastern part of the island in particular.

The form of Ireland's relationship with Britain has thus been one of the constant, defining features of the modern Irish experience, north and south, but the fluctuating fortunes of that relationship should not obscure the more nuanced but equally interesting links which have been forged between

Ireland and the wider world over the course of the last century and a half. The most tangible of those bonds have come in the shape of its people, the hundreds of thousands of emigrants who, for a variety of reasons, left their homeland to seek a new life elsewhere. Many of these, particularly during the middle of the 20th century, settled in the neighbouring isle but for the earlier period and again more recently other, more distant destinations have figured prominently — most obviously in America but also in Canada, Australia, New Zealand and elsewhere. Not that their departure meant that

Below: *Charles Haughey, the most charismatic and controversial Irish Taoiseach of modern times.*

they or their offspring lost interest in matters affecting the 'mother country'; on the contrary, these communities sustained a vibrant sense of Irish nationality in their adopted homes, albeit one attenuated by the conditions of the host society.

In addition to the legacy of the Irish abroad, numerous bonds have also served to incorporate the Irish experience into that of mainland Europe during these eventful years, a mutual interaction given institutional recognition in 1973 with the entry of both the Republic of Ireland and Northern Ireland (as part of the United Kingdom) into the European Economic Community (subsequently the European Union). It is the economic impact of this association which has, perhaps not surprisingly, received the lion's share of attention over the last quarter of a century but this should not blind one to its powerful social and political undercurrents — undercurrents which may, in the fullness of time, come to be regarded as its most enduring legacy.

It is, however, the story of what happened, and those who remained, in Ireland with which we are most concerned here. In this respect the transfer of political power from London to administrations in both Dublin and (to a lesser extent) Belfast in the early 1920s provided an opportunity for these governments to formulate policies designed to promote the specific interests of the Irish people. The development of two distinctive socio-political regimes north and south of the border — the former self-consciously British and Protestant, the latter explicitly Gaelic and Catholic in its cultural formation — bore testimony to the deep divisions within the country which predated even the Famine, but even here the enduring ties of history between the two political areas should not be ignored. It is one of the enduring ironies of modern Irish history that the regional differences within the island — east/west as well as north/south — are in many respects less manifest now than in the middle of the 19th century, but are widely known and more

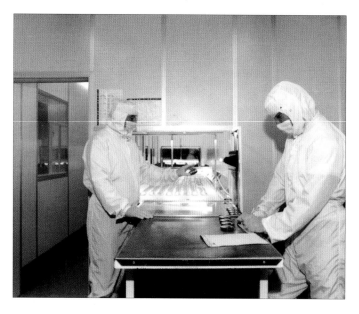

Above and right: *During the late 1980s and 1990s Ireland has enjoyed outstanding economic success, growing consistently around 6/7%. The high standard of education has attracted inward investment from the global economy, backed by infrastructural investment from the EU. The establishment of new activities, such as computers and financial services, has led to an increasing sophistication and diversification of opportunity, alongside Ireland's traditional and well established industries.*

keenly felt, and it is in this context that the debate on national identify, the nature of the Irish quintessence, which has proliferated over the last century, must be studied.

In short, while the island of Ireland has undoubtedly experienced massive and at times painful social and political change since 1851, evidence of the pervasive influence of its historical inheritance is as much in evidence on its contemporary intellectual landscape as it is on its physical one.

Post-Famine Emigration

THE FAMINE was a milestone in modern Irish history, not merely because of the sheer horror of the human suffering it carried in its wake (awful though this was) but also because it gave an added impetus to the development of profound social changes which had become evident during the years immediately prior to 1845.

Of these changes it was perhaps the scale of emigration which was the most important. So huge was this emigration that Ireland, which had experienced substantial population expansion over the course of the previous 100 years, now entered a period of population decline which had no contemporary comparison in Europe and which was to continue almost unchecked for well over a century. This phenomenon affected all creeds and classes and touched all parts of the country, although the poorer elements of the Catholic agricultural population of the south and west manifested the greatest relative decline, with Munster experiencing the largest absolute losses. The scale of female emigration was particularly noticeable, with the number of female emigrants at times outnumbering their male counterparts (contrary to the experience of most other countries).

While some emigrants settled in the growing industrial towns across the Irish Sea, most found themselves embarked on the hazardous sea journey towards a new life in North America, and in particular the United States. Initially finding themselves the subject of suspicion and distrust in their adopted homeland they nonetheless quickly adjusted and made an enormous contribution to the subsequent development of the country. Notwithstanding the fact that they had in the main come from an agricultural background, most of these emigrants settled in large cities on the east coast of America, and while the numbers returning to Ireland remained small in comparison to other nationalities, yet they retained an interest in Irish affairs which has persisted to the present day.

Back in Ireland other important demographic trends were becoming noticeable. In particular the marriage rate, which had been quite high prior to the Famine, now slowly declined (although as can be seen from the map this process did not proceed at the same pace throughout the island). This was due to the increase in the number of individuals who never married, together with an increase in the average age at the time. Notwithstanding this significant development the birth rate remained well above the European average, although this was also subject to significant geographic variation.

Below: 'Steerage emigrants', a wood engraving by Arthur Boyd Houghton, published in the Graphic, *March 1869, shows poor emigrants sailing the cheap steerage passage to North America.*

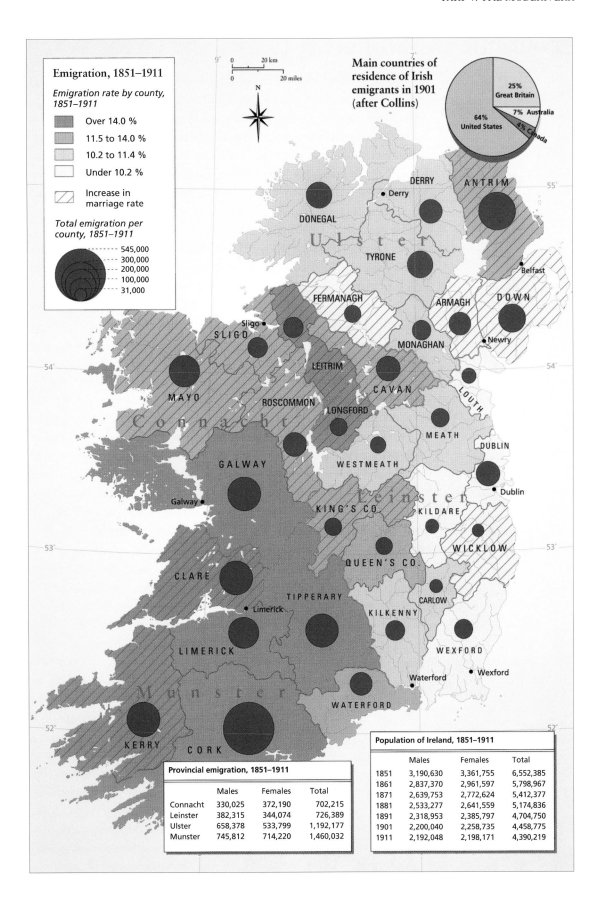

Emigration, 1851–1911

Emigration rate by county, 1851–1911

▓	Over 14.0 %
▓	11.5 to 14.0 %
░	10.2 to 11.4 %
☐	Under 10.2 %
▨	Increase in marriage rate

Total emigration per county, 1851–1911

545,000
300,000
200,000
100,000
31,000

Main countries of residence of Irish emigrants in 1901 (after Collins)

64% United States
25% Great Britain
7% Australia
4% Canada

0   20 km
0   20 miles
N

9°   7°
55°
54°
53°
52°

DERRY
• Derry
ANTRIM
DONEGAL
Ulster
TYRONE
• Belfast
FERMANAGH
ARMAGH
DOWN
Sligo •
SLIGO
MONAGHAN
• Newry
MAYO
LEITRIM
Connacht
ROSCOMMON
CAVAN
LOUTH
LONGFORD
MEATH
Galway •
GALWAY
WESTMEATH
DUBLIN
Leinster
KING'S CO.
KILDARE
• Dublin
QUEEN'S CO.
WICKLOW
CLARE
TIPPERARY
• Limerick
KILKENNY
CARLOW
LIMERICK
WEXFORD
Munster
WATERFORD
• Wexford
Waterford •
KERRY
CORK

Provincial emigration, 1851–1911

	Males	Females	Total
Connacht	330,025	372,190	702,215
Leinster	382,315	344,074	726,389
Ulster	658,378	533,799	1,192,177
Munster	745,812	714,220	1,460,032

Population of Ireland, 1851–1911

	Males	Females	Total
1851	3,190,630	3,361,755	6,552,385
1861	2,837,370	2,961,597	5,798,967
1871	2,639,753	2,772,624	5,412,377
1881	2,533,277	2,641,559	5,174,836
1891	2,318,953	2,385,797	4,704,750
1901	2,200,040	2,258,735	4,458,775
1911	2,192,048	2,198,171	4,390,219

Economic Development before the Great War

THE HUMAN changes which followed the Famine were accompanied (and indeed partly explained) by dramatic changes in the national economy. One of the most important of these was the acceleration of the shift in agricultural production away from small-scale intensive tillage operations towards a more extensive dairy system. There were many reasons for this development, which involved the frequently controversial consolidation of large numbers of small holdings into more substantial and efficient units. Undoubtedly the Irish climate played a part, being conducive to grazing, but the government also exercised a direct influence, particularly by means of the legislation which it passed in the aftermath of the Famine which simplified the rather cumbersome existing procedures for the transfer of the ownership of land.

Such chances, together with the now near-universal tendency for land to be inherited en bloc rather than be divided up among competing offspring, produced large numbers of individuals and families who could find no role in the new economic dispensation and who formed the bulk of the emigrants discussed earlier. In the north, however, the second major development in the Irish economy during the second part of the century — the growth of manufacturing industry in the area (particularly in Belfast and Derry) — provided for many an alternative to the emigrant ship. Large numbers of agricultural workers, both Catholic and Protestant, now settled in these cities, hoping to find work in the new ship-building yards or linen mills which were opening at that time. These workers frequently had to endure appalling working and living conditions, to which were added the tensions which had long characterized relations between the two major religious blocs in the area.

A number of other developments in the national economy must also be mentioned. In particular the Irish economy was becoming ever more integrated into the British economic sphere of influence, a development aided by the improved road, rail and port facilities which developed in the 60 years after the Famine. Irish economic activity generally became more commercially-oriented and moved decisively away from the subsistence-type of production which had characterized certain areas in the earlier decades of the century. Partly as a consequence of this development, living standards across the island gradually improved, although it did leave the economy rather vulnerable to changes in European and world markets over which it had little control.

Below: Shipyard workers leaving the Harland and Wolff yard in Belfast at the end of a working day. Belfast and its environs were the centre of Ireland's industrial revolution, thus marking the north off even more from the agricultural south and west.

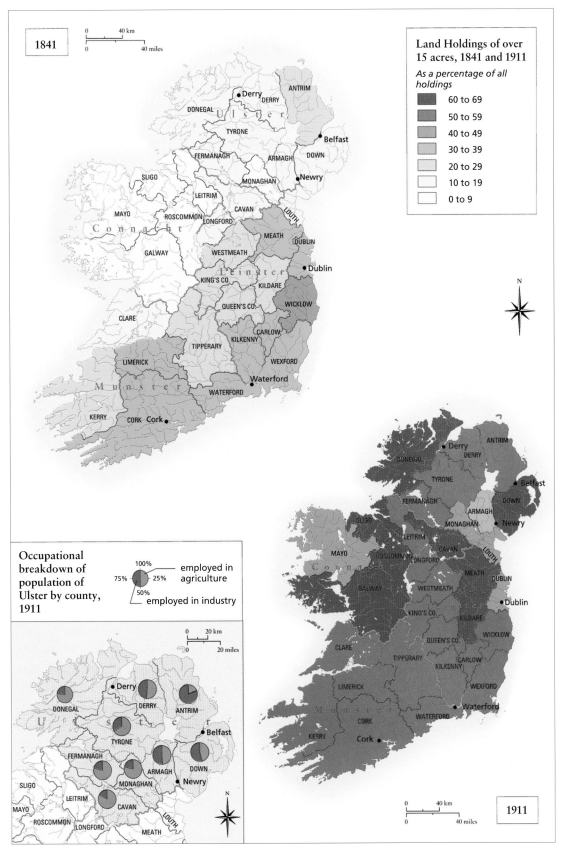

1841

0   40 km
0   40 miles

**Land Holdings of over
15 acres, 1841 and 1911**

*As a percentage of all
holdings*

- 60 to 69
- 50 to 59
- 40 to 49
- 30 to 39
- 20 to 29
- 10 to 19
- 0 to 9

**Occupational
breakdown of
population of
Ulster by county,
1911**

100%
75%   25%
50%

employed in
agriculture

employed in industry

0   20 km
0   20 miles

1911

0   40 km
0   40 miles

The Growth of Irish Nationalism

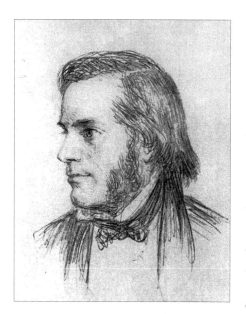

Above: *Thomas Davis, editor of*
The Nation, *was a popular idealist and the chief ideologue of the Young Ireland movement.*

THE TRAUMA of the Famine and the consequent readjustments provided an important impetus to the growth of political and cultural nationalism in the country. Building on the foundations laid by the United Irishmen and Daniel O'Connell, a series of individuals and groups during the latter part of the 19th century sought to cultivate a nationalist consciousness which would be the precursor to new and distinctively Irish political and social arrangements.

The first of these bodies — the Young Ireland movement of the 1840s — provided a coherent if not necessarily programmatic doctrine of nationality which was to inspire later generations. After failed rebellions in 1848 and 1867, it was only in the 1870s and 1880s that demands for the recognition of Ireland's distinctive inheritance found practical political expression through the activities at Westminster of the Irish Parliamentary Party, under the leadership initially of Isaac Butt and subsequently (and most impressively) of Charles Stewart Parnell. That both these men were Protestants bestowed upon the movement a deceptively ecumenical façade — in practice Irish nationalism became increasingly defined with the majority Catholic community (a development mirrored by the growth in support amongst Protestants for the maintenance of the Union of 1800).

A number of gains were made by the Irish Party, particularly in the area of land reform which the government undertook in the hope that it would forestall the growth of separatist sentiment, but on the key issue of political reform no progress was made and the controversial downfall of Parnell following his involvement in a divorce case seemed to stymie such hopes for the foreseeable future. Some felt that such a development was the inevitable consequence of constitutional action, and a revolutionary wing to the nationalist movement, the Irish Republican Brotherhood (the 'Fenians') was developed, albeit with little overt popular support.

It was, however, not just in political terms that the new sense of nationality manifested itself. Developments such as the foundation of the Gaelic Athletic Association (1884), a body dedicated to the maintenance of traditional Irish sports, and of the Gaelic League (1893), which sought to stem the apparently inexorable decline of the Irish language, bore testimony to a dynamic perception of nationality independent of political arrangements, a perception which found enduring cultural expression in the varied works of the Irish 'literary renaissance' evident during these years. The foundation in 1905 of Sinn Féin, a broadly-based nationalist organisation with a distinctive economic agenda, was but the latest in a long line of such bodies, although it was arguably to become the most influential in the renewed drive towards political independence.

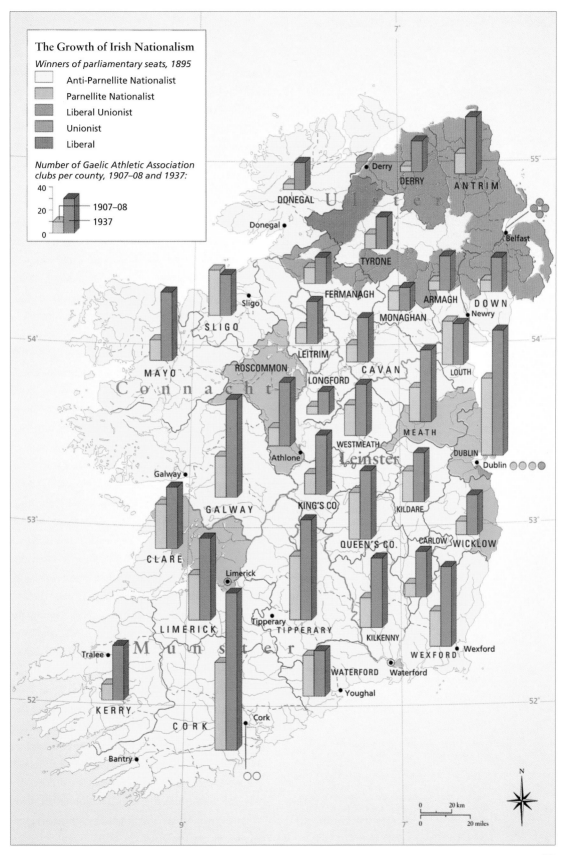

The Growth of Irish Nationalism

Winners of parliamentary seats, 1895

- Anti-Parnellite Nationalist
- Parnellite Nationalist
- Liberal Unionist
- Unionist
- Liberal

Number of Gaelic Athletic Association clubs per county, 1907–08 and 1937:

40

20

0

1907–08

1937

Government Policy

Above: *This well-known staged photograph features a means rarely used in case of eviction for non-payment of rent: the battering ram.*

THE GROWTH of nationalist sentiment presented the British government with severe difficulties. On the one hand the refusal to make concessions to the burgeoning nationalist lobby ran the risk of alienating the moderate majority; on the other, to give in to such demands raised the possibility of further, perhaps unpalatable demands.

The government's response had two elements. On the one hand it enacted wide-ranging social reforms where these were deemed to be compatible with existing constitutional arrangements. These reforms included the Land Acts (which essentially transferred ownership from landlord to tenant), the disestablishment of the Church of Ireland (1869), the establishment of a number of state agencies to assist with the task of developing the poorest areas of the country, and so on. In its latter stages this policy was accurately described as 'killing Home Rule by kindness', that is, the removal of the social grievances which were felt to underpin the demand for political separation.

However the government proved itself willing to employ coercive methods whenever the political situation became unacceptably tense. This strategy was particularly evident during the so-called 'Land War' of 1879-82, when a number of individuals and organizations, notably the 'Land League' led by Michael Davitt, were the object of official harassment, and also during the 'Plan of Campaign' from 1886-92, which also focused on the key issue of land reform.

Two attempts were made to find a solution to the political question. In 1885 Gladstone, the Liberal Prime Minister, introduced a 'Home Rule' Bill, which sought to bestow very limited powers on an all-Ireland Parliament. Even this was too much for Conservatives and Unionists, who launched a vigorous campaign of opposition to the Bill, which was defeated when the Liberal Party split on the issue in 1886. A second attempt by Gladstone to pass the Bill failed in 1893 when the measure was vetoed by the Conservative-dominated House of Lords.

For the next 20 years the Home Rule issue dropped off a political agenda dominated by the ruling Conservative Party, and attention in Ireland switched to social and economic issues. However the political and emotional capital invested in Home Rule by both Irish nationalists and British Liberals meant that the return of that latter party to power would inevitably witness a resurgence of interest in the question.

Land Legislation, 1870–1903

1870	*Made customary tenant right enforceable at law and provided compensation for disturbance.*
1881	*Concession of the 'Three Fs': right of free sale; judicial power to fix rents; conversion of ordinary tenancies to fixed tenancies.*
1885	*Allowed land commission to lend to tenants to purchase holdings from landlords.*
1903	*Wyndham's Act. Provided for long-term low-interest government loans to buy out landlords' interests. This crucial piece of legislation effectively ended the land question and created the typical 20th-century pattern of independent family farms.*

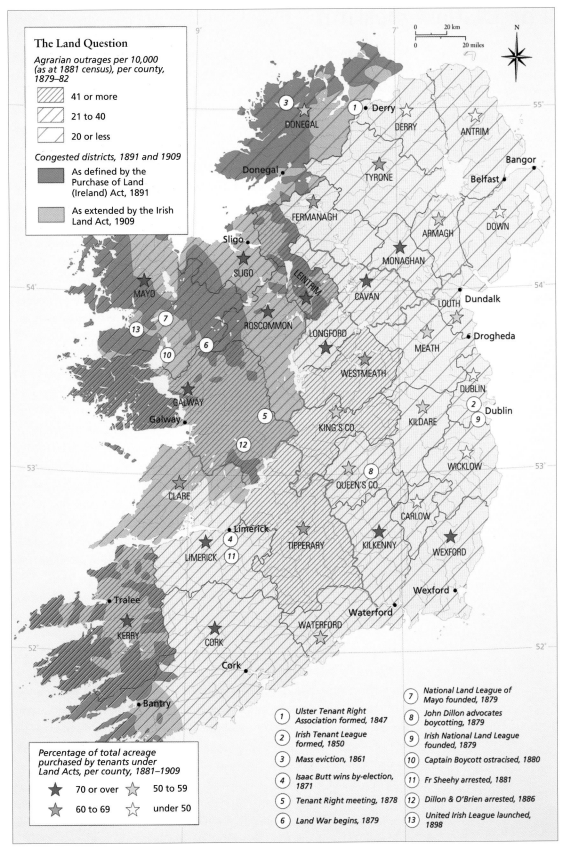

The Land Question

Agrarian outrages per 10,000 (as at 1881 census), per county, 1879–82

- 41 or more
- 21 to 40
- 20 or less

Congested districts, 1891 and 1909

- As defined by the Purchase of Land (Ireland) Act, 1891
- As extended by the Irish Land Act, 1909

Percentage of total acreage purchased by tenants under Land Acts, per county, 1881–1909

- 70 or over
- 60 to 69
- 50 to 59
- under 50

1. Ulster Tenant Right Association formed, 1847
2. Irish Tenant League formed, 1850
3. Mass eviction, 1861
4. Isaac Butt wins by-election, 1871
5. Tenant Right meeting, 1878
6. Land War begins, 1879
7. National Land League of Mayo founded, 1879
8. John Dillon advocates boycotting, 1879
9. Irish National Land League founded, 1879
10. Captain Boycott ostracised, 1880
11. Fr Sheehy arrested, 1881
12. Dillon & O'Brien arrested, 1886
13. United Irish League launched, 1898

The Ulster Question

IT WAS IN 1912 that the British government, once more led by a Liberal prime minister and supported by the votes of the Irish Parliamentary Party, returned to the issue of Home Rule. The terms of the Bill introduced in April of that year were similar to earlier proposals, but provoked an even more hostile response from its opponents, particularly in Ulster.

There were several reasons why the campaign of opposition to Home Rule during 1912–14 was markedly more bitter than those of the previous generation. The Liberal Party had been shorn of its unionist wing and so a repetition of the internal divisions of 1886 was not to be expected; the veto of the House of Lords had been removed some years earlier, so a repeat of the disappointment of 1893 was impossible; and unionist support had become more concentrated in Ulster, the area of Ireland with the highest concentration of Protestants, than theretofore, when the opposition had been characterized by an all-Ireland dimension.

Led by such men as Edward Carson and James Craig, the campaign became increasingly bellicose in tone. Actions during 1912–14 such as the signing of the Solemn League and Covenant, the formation of the Ulster Volunteer Force and the Larne gun-running signalled a determination at all costs to maintain the Union intact; and when allied with other developments such as the Curragh 'mutiny' and the formation of the opposing National Volunteers, the situation in Ulster seemed to threaten the possibility of civil war.

The Ulster Question

- Counties with Catholic majority, 1911 census
- Counties with Protestant majority, 1911 census
- Limit of Northern Ireland, Government of Ireland Act, 1920
- Limit of historic Ulster province

The crisis was temporarily 'solved' by the outbreak of war in Europe in August 1914, with the Bill being passed by parliament but being suspended for the duration of hostilities. Perhaps more importantly provision was also made for the possibility of special treatment for Ulster as compared to the rest of the country. The exclusion of some or all of the nine counties of Ulster from the terms of the Bill had been bitterly opposed by nationalists, although John Redmond, leader of the Irish Parliamentary Party, had been willing to concede the principle of temporary exclusion of certain counties in order to secure the passage of the Bill as a whole. The failure adequately to resolve the objections of Ulster unionists, however, was to have fatal consequences when the question was re-examined, in even more unfavourable conditions, after the end of the war in Europe.

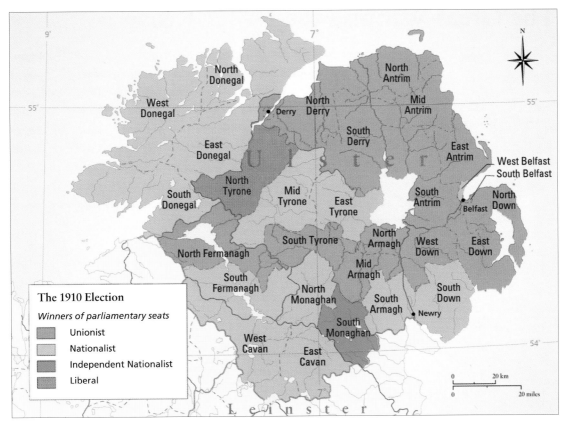

The 1910 Election

Winners of parliamentary seats

- Unionist
- Nationalist
- Independent Nationalist
- Liberal

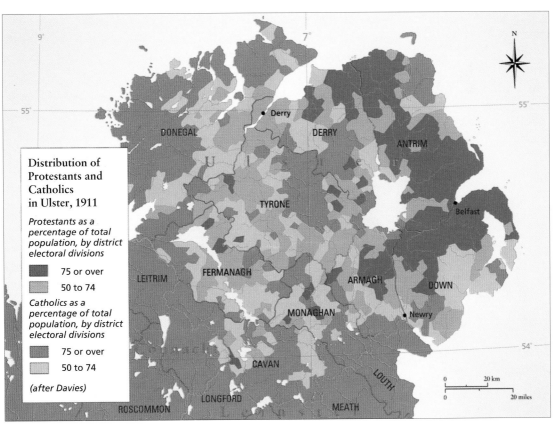

Distribution of Protestants and Catholics in Ulster, 1911

Protestants as a percentage of total population, by district electoral divisions

- 75 or over
- 50 to 74

Catholics as a percentage of total population, by district electoral divisions

- 75 or over
- 50 to 74

(after Davies)

The Great War and the Easter Rising

Above: Éamon de Valera, commander of the rebel garrison in Boland's Mills, under arrest and escorted by British troops, Dublin, 1916.

IN COMMON with the rest of Europe the 'Great War' of 1914–18 had far-reaching consequences for Ireland. The human dimension of Ireland's contribution to the war effort was enormous, with over 270,000 men (40per cent of the adult male population) serving in the British armed forces, and many thousands more working in the new munitions factories. The front line soldiers were to endure the same horrifying conditions as the other combatants, and casualties also reached the same appalling levels — barely a village escaped those years without the death of at least one local young man, with particularly savage losses being inflicted at the battle of the Somme in July 1916.

These human sufferings had a political as well as a military dimension. Many of the large numbers of nationalists who enlisted did so because they felt that their actions would serve to guarantee Home Rule for Ireland; conversely members of the Ulster Volunteer Force who volunteered felt that their sacrifices would be sufficient to ensure the defeat of the same measure. The apparent preference shown by the British government to the claims of the latter group added to the sense of discontent within the ranks of radical nationalist opinion, a discontent which was to become manifest with the events of the Easter Rising of April 1916.

This insurrection, which lasted less than a week, was fatally hindered by poor planning, inappropriate tactics and sheer bad luck. As a consequence of divisions within the leadership of the movement the Rising, which was originally intended to encompass the entire country, was concentrated almost entirely in the centre of Dublin. In spite of the personal bravery shown by many of the insurgents, the outcome of the drama was never really in doubt and on Saturday 29 April an unconditional surrender was signed by the leaders of the Volunteers, after a mere six days of fighting.

Below: After the battle, citizens of Dublin walk through the rubble-strewn streets, the painful aftermath of the 1916 Easter Rising.

In military terms the Rising was an unmitigated disaster for the Volunteers — casualties were high, with all those not killed or injured being interned by the British, and all of the munitions so painstakingly stockpiled being lost in a few short days. What the Rising did signal, however, through the actions and rhetoric of figures as diverse as Pádraig Pearse and James Connolly, was a militancy which could not be accommodated within the old Home Rule framework, and which was to become a determining factor in the Irish political scene over the next seven years.

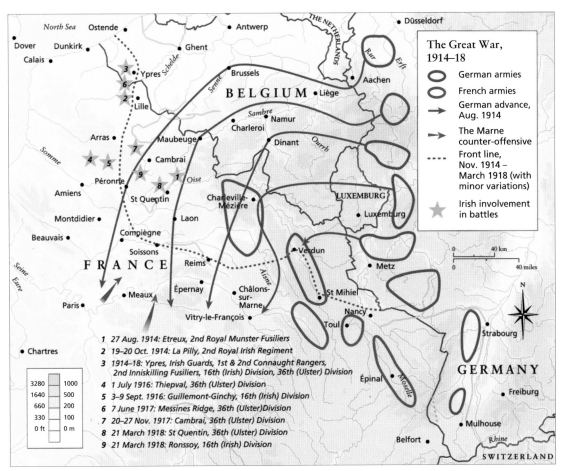

The Great War, 1914–18

- **German armies**
- **French armies**
- **→** German advance, Aug. 1914
- **→** The Marne counter-offensive
- **----** Front line, Nov. 1914 – March 1918 (with minor variations)
- **★** Irish involvement in battles

1 27 Aug. 1914: Etreux, 2nd Royal Munster Fusiliers
2 19–20 Oct. 1914: La Pilly, 2nd Royal Irish Regiment
3 1914–18: Ypres, Irish Guards, 1st & 2nd Connaught Rangers, 2nd Inniskilling Fusiliers, 16th (Irish) Division, 36th (Ulster) Division
4 1 July 1916: Thiepval, 36th (Ulster) Division
5 3–9 Sept. 1916: Guillemont-Ginchy, 16th (Irish) Division
6 7 June 1917: Messines Ridge, 36th (Ulster) Division
7 20–27 Nov. 1917: Cambrai, 36th (Ulster) Division
8 21 March 1918: St Quentin, 36th (Ulster) Division
9 21 March 1918: Ronssoy, 16th (Irish) Division

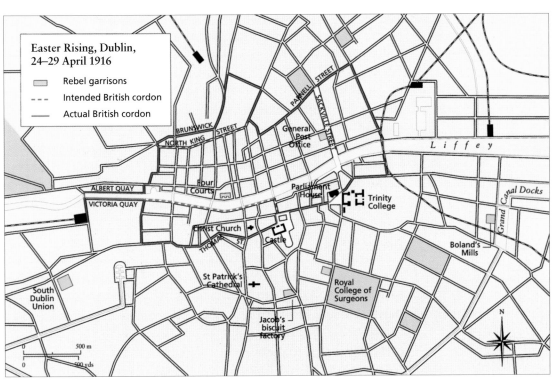

Easter Rising, Dublin, 24–29 April 1916

- Rebel garrisons
- **----** Intended British cordon
- **——** Actual British cordon

Separation 1916–23

Above: *King George V opening the first parliament of the new Northern Ireland on 21 June 1921.*

NATIONALIST MILITANCY was compounded by serious government errors in the aftermath of the Rising, such as the execution of the leaders of the Rising and an ill-judged proposal to introduce conscription. It gained further momentum during 1917–18, with reorganizations both of the Volunteer movement (now known as Irish Republican Army) and of Sinn Féin, which now became the main vehicle for the expression of radical nationalist sentiment. The party's sweeping victory in the 1918 General Election, where it dominated the vote outside much of Ulster, gave added momentum to the separatist effort.

This momentum was consolidated by the foundation of Dáil Eireann, a republican assembly, in January 1919 and by the commencement in the same month of a vigorous guerrilla war undertaken by the IRA. Over the course of the next two years a number of violent incidents occurred, including 'Bloody Sunday' (marked by the deaths of 23 soldiers and civilians), the burning of Cork City and the destruction of the Custom House in Dublin. In an effort to stem the activities of the IRA the government introduced a number of specially-recruited and ruthlessly aggressive units into Ireland, most notoriously the so-called 'Black and Tans', but the excesses of these units only served to diminish further the moral authority of the government in the face of world opinion. A truce between the two sides was brokered during July 1921, following the formal partition of the country and the establishment of Northern Ireland under the Government of Ireland Act, and some months later a republican negotiating team was dispatched to London, led by Arthur Griffith and Michael Collins.

The 'Treaty' signed by this delegation with the British government in December 1921 was unacceptable to many republicans, who felt that it did not fully recognize Ireland's legitimate claim for independence. Prominent amongst these dissenters was Éamon de Valera, who had led the underground republican Government during the War of Independence. These disagreements erupted into Civil War in June 1922, with an attack by the Provisional Government established by the terms of the Treaty on the republican-held Four Courts in Dublin. The next 12 months saw widespread unrest, with the deaths of many leading figures on both sides, but in truth government victory was rarely in doubt. What was in doubt, however, was the ability of the new 'Irish Free State' to overcome the severe problems facing it as a young European state.

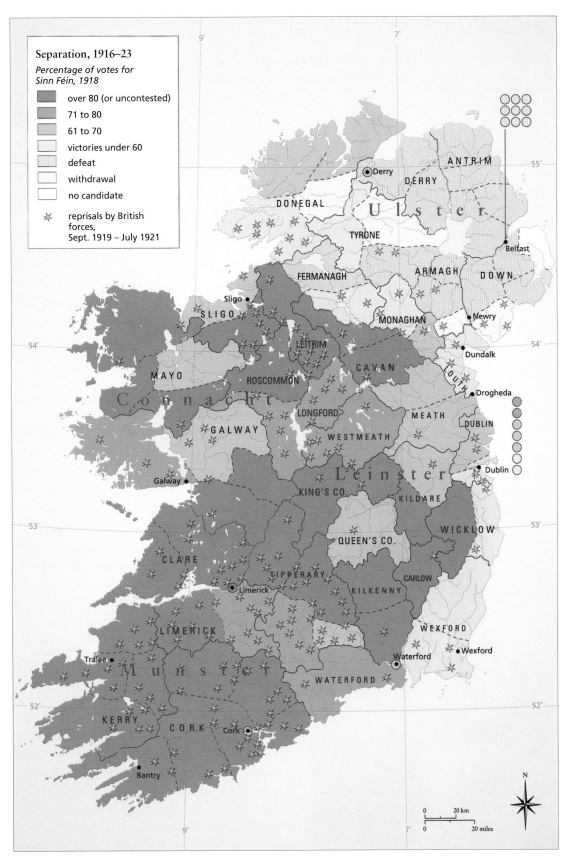

Separation, 1916–23

Percentage of votes for
Sinn Féin, 1918

- over 80 (or uncontested)
- 71 to 80
- 61 to 70
- victories under 60
- defeat
- withdrawal
- no candidate

✳ reprisals by British forces, Sept. 1919 – July 1921

Cumann na nGaedheal

HAVING PREVAILED in the Civil War the Cumann na nGaedheal government, which was composed of Treaty supporters under the leadership of W.T. Cosgrave, now embarked on a comprehensive political, social and economic programme designed both to promote stability and growth in the country and also to consolidate its own electoral position.

In the main the government's programme was characterized by cautious continuity rather than daring innovation. In terms of the structure of the civil service, legal system, police force, army, and the education system it was content to follow the broad principles laid down by the British administration. In economic affairs continuity was also the hallmark. The government completed the process of buying out the landlords but in most other respects refused to intervene directly in the economy, although its support for the Shannon hydroelectric scheme for example demonstrated a willingness to undertake substantial projects where necessary. Ireland remained, however, a predominantly agricultural country, with most exports destined for Britain from whom she in return imported most of her manufactured goods. Taxation remained low but poverty was rife.

The government also pursued a cautious line in its foreign policy, building up a small diplomatic corps in Europe and America but concentrating on the crucial relationship with Great Britain. The issue of Northern Ireland was a persistent problem, with the border between north and south being only finally ratified in 1925, when the Boundary Commission established under the Treaty collapsed in chaos. While the government was keen to maintain good relations with the British government it also sought to consolidate its own freedom of action, and it played an important role in the Commonwealth Conferences during these years.

Internal security remained a problem, however. A potential mutiny in the Army was averted in 1924, while the defeat of the IRA in the Civil War had not removed the threat of republican sedition. De Valera was frustrated by the rather sterile abstentionist policies of Sinn Féin and founded his own party, Fianna Fáil, in 1926. In the following year he led his followers into the Free State Dáil when it appeared that the government was trying to exclude them permanently following the assassination of Kevin O'Higgins, a leading government minister.

Cumann na nGaedheal managed to hang on to power for five more years, but following the General Election of 1932 Fianna Fáil was able to form a minority government and set about implementing its radical manifesto.

Below: William Thomas Cosgrave, President of the Irish Free State, making a speech in 1922. The new government had a dual task of rebuilding the country after the struggle for freedom and providing politically for the nation's desire for independence with unity.

The Anti-Treaty Vote in the General Election, 1923

– – – proposed change of border

Percentage of first-preference votes for Sinn Féin (anti-Treaty)

31 or over

21 to 30

14 to 20

① January 1923: establishment of Garda training camp

② March 1924: army 'mutiny'

③ 1926: establishment of state power company

④ May 1926: public launch of Fianna Fáil

⑤ July 1927: assassination of Kevin O'Higgins

⑥ August 1927: entry of Fianna Fáil into Dáil

⑦ Establishment of state broadcasting system: 1926 Dublin, 1927 Cork, 1932 Athlone

⑧ July 1929: opening of Shannon hydroelectric scheme

⑨ 1931: IRA Wolfe Tone commemoration prohibited

Fianna Fáil

ON COMING to power in 1932 de Valera immediately set about the task of realizing his distinctive view of national development. One of his first actions was to suspend the payment of land annuities by Irish farmers to the British overnment, which led through a series of retaliatory measures into a full-scale 'Economic War', characterised on both sides by severe protectionist measures. De Valera seized on this opportunity to develop small domestic industries, although the damage to the agricultural sector, particularly to the small farmer group which formed the backbone of the party's rural vote, led to the gradual decline of the policy in the late 1930s.

In other areas too de Valera sought to influence Irish social development, particularly in the areas of education policy, Church-State relations and Anglo-Irish affairs. This latter issue was especially problematic, but by degrees the Cabinet succeeded in removing the most objectionable elements of the 1921 Treaty (particularly the Oath of Alliegance and the Office of Governor-General) and in 1937 de Valera successfully introduced a new Constitution.

The democratic tone of this Constitution was noteworthy at a time when fascism was at its height in Europe. Following an agreement with Great Britain in 1938, which ended the 'Economic War' and returned to Irish control several ports hitherto the responsibility of the Royal Navy, de Valera adopted a policy of military neutrality during the Second World War (or 'Emergency' as it was called in Ireland). The maintenance of this policy in spite of pressures both from the Allies (particularly after the entry of America into the War) and from Nazi Germany was a major diplomatic undertaking, one which required the government to take severe action against their former republican comrades in arms (de Valera had, in fact, immediately on coming to power, suppressed the quite distinct and quasi-fascist 'Blueshirt' movement in the country). In practice his policies favoured the Allies, but his formal adherence to neutrality gained the country few friends abroad.

The government found itself increasingly unpopular after the end of the War, when a combination of continued economic hardship, the emergence of new rival political parties and a series of scandals combined to present the image of a party too long in power. Its defeat in the 1948 election, however, only served to draw attention to the momentous changes witnessed during the previous 16 years.

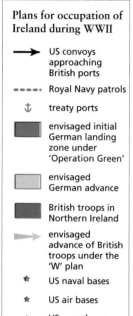

Plans for occupation of Ireland during WWII

→ US convoys approaching British ports

---- Royal Navy patrols

⚓ treaty ports

▓ envisaged initial German landing zone under 'Operation Green'

▢ envisaged German advance

▓ British troops in Northern Ireland

➤ envisaged advance of British troops under the 'W' plan

✦ US naval bases

★ US air bases

☆ US army bases

0 40 km
0 40 miles

Fianna Fáil

Percentage of first-preference votes for Fianna Fáil, 1932

- 51 or over
- 41 to 50
- 31 to 40
- 30 or under

Distribution of agricultural holdings, by province, 1932

LEINSTER

MUNSTER

CONNACHT

Number of holdings in thousands

Size of holdings in acres

The '40s and '50s: Turmoil and Malaise

THE 1950s in Ireland were characterized above all by severe economic difficulties, difficulties which were exacerbated by the political instability of the period. Having only experienced two, single-party governments during the first 25 years of the state's existence, three short lived governments (two 'inter-party' coalitions and one Fianna Fáil minority administration) now followed each other in quick succession. None of these cabinets was able to get to grips with the enormous problems facing the country during the period, although in 1949 the first inter-party government did take the dramatic step of formally declaring a Republic. The political scene during these years was dominated by a number of crises, most famously the 'Mother and Child' debacle of 1951, when a proposal to reform the health care provided to expectant mothers and young children collapsed amidst political indecision and pressure from the Catholic Church and the medical profession.

Such a political situation provided a decidedly unhelpful context in which to address the enormous economic problems facing the country. Foremost amongst these was a resurgence in emigration, which reached levels not witnessed since the 1880s and which came to symbolize the failure of the Irish state to provide a basic standard of living for its citizens, contrary to the hopes and expectations of those who had campaigned so hard for its independence. This increase in emigrants was due to a combination of factors, most notably the increasing use of machinery in rural areas which reduced the demand for farm labour, the lack of indigenous industrial development in urban centres and the enormous demand for labour in the major industrial centres in Britain. All these factors conspired to siphon off enormous numbers of young Irish men and women, with the poverty-stricken areas of the western seaboard being particularly badly affected.

While some efforts were made to arrest this loss of population, which was accentuated by a decline in the marriage rate, there was little scope for innovative policy given the restrictions imposed by the prevailing economic orthodoxies. It was only with the election in 1959 of Seán Lemass as Taoiseach and leader of Fianna Fáil in succession to de Valera (who was subsequently elected to two terms as President of Ireland) that the almost hermetically-sealed nature of the Irish economy and society was finally opened up to external influences.

Death rate from Tuberculosis, 1950–54

- Increase
- Decrease up to 30%
- Decrease from 31 to 60%
- Decrease over 60%

Northern Ireland
Subject to U.K. National Health organization founded 1946

DONEGAL · SLIGO · LEITRIM · MAYO · ROSCOMMON · CAVAN · MONAGHAN · LOUTH · Connacht · LONGFORD · MEATH · WESTMEATH · DUBLIN · GALWAY · Leinster · OFFALY · KILDARE · LAOIS · WICKLOW · CLARE · CARLOW · TIPPERARY · KILKENNY · LIMERICK · WEXFORD · Munster · KERRY · WATERFORD · CORK

0   40 km
0   40 miles

N

Estimated annual emigration from Northern Ireland, 1954–61

Net emigration in thousands

1954 55 56 57 58 59 60 61

Years

Population change, 1926–61

Percentage of population change, per county

Increase

+10 or over

0 to 10

Decrease

-10 to 0

-20 to -11

-21 or under

Inter-censal emigration from the Republic of Ireland, 1926–61

Emigrants per 1000 population (*red line*)

166,751   187,111   119,568   196,763   212,003

1926   36   46   51   56   61

Inter-censal period

Northern Ireland

Above: *James Craig, Lord Craigavon, the first Prime Minister of Northern Ireland.*

By the late 1950s the six county 'statelet' of Northern Ireland, established under the 1920 Government of Ireland Act, had also performed very badly in terms of social and economic development. One of the reasons for this stagnation was the nature of the original political settlement. Born out of Unionist opposition both to Home Rule and republican separatism, the territory encompassed by the state was a compromise between the historic nine county province of Ulster and the four counties where Protestants enjoyed numerical superiority over the Catholic community. The presence of substantial Catholic communities in border areas presented the new government (led by Sir James Craig) with severe difficulties, particularly during the years 1922–23 which were marked by severe communal violence. The confirmation of the border in 1925, by means of a tripartite agreement with the Free State and British cabinets (in return for which Dublin received financial concessions) meant that the Unionist government in Belfast was free to turn its attention to the consolidation of state and party interests.

Almost immediately complaints began to emerge regarding the abuse of the rights of the Catholic/nationalist minority. These complaints were concentrated in particular on electoral arrangements, which, it was suggested, were manipulated in the interests of the Unionist Party; on public and private employment, which Catholics alleged was characterized by severe religious discrimination; on security arrangements, which seemed at times geared more towards the suppression of political dissent rather than criminal activity; and on education, where, for a number of reasons Catholic schools received less financial assistance than their state-sponsored Protestant counterparts. While some of these grievances may have been exaggerated it seems clear that the political aspirations of the general Catholic community were regarded with hostility at the highest levels of the Northern state.

The decision of the Stormont government to participate in the Second World War drove a further wedge between it and neutral Éire. The experience of wartime industrial and military mobilization, and the tragedy of the Belfast Blitz, inevitably placed an emotional distance between north and south, a distance confirmed by the 1949 Ireland Act, which guaranteed the maintenance of the state so long as it enjoyed majority support. Notwithstanding the poor economic performance of the 1950s there seemed little danger that the government, now headed by Sir Basil Brooke, was in any danger of losing such support.

Below: *Inter-communal violence has a long and depressing history in Northern Ireland. This newspaper headline dates from 1935, at which time the tradition of civil unrest was already almost a century old.*

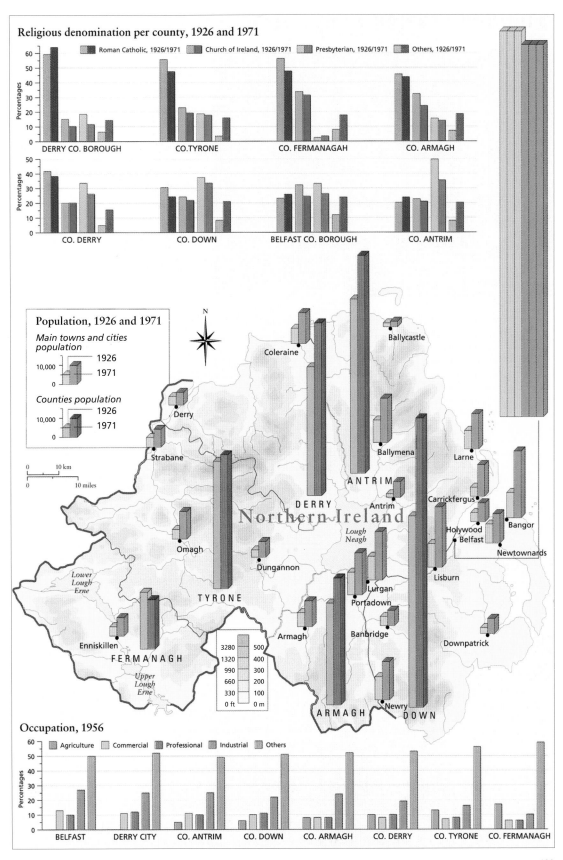

Religious denomination per county, 1926 and 1971

Roman Catholic, 1926/1971   Church of Ireland, 1926/1971   Presbyterian, 1926/1971   Others, 1926/1971

Percentages

DERRY CO. BOROUGH   CO.TYRONE   CO. FERMANAGAH   CO. ARMAGH

CO. DERRY   CO. DOWN   BELFAST CO. BOROUGH   CO. ANTRIM

Population, 1926 and 1971

Main towns and cities population

10,000   1926   1971

0

Counties population

10,000   1926   1971

0

N

Coleraine

Ballycastle

Derry

Strabane

Ballymena

Larne

ANTRIM

DERRY

Antrim

Carrickfergus

0   10 km
0   10 miles

Northern Ireland

Holywood

Bangor

Omagh

Lough Neagh

Belfast

Newtownards

Dungannon

Lisburn

Lower Lough Erne

TYRONE

Lurgan

Portadown

Armagh

Banbridge

Downpatrick

Enniskillen

FERMANAGH

Upper Lough Erne

3280   500
1320   400
990   300
660   200
330   100
0 ft   0 m

Newry

ARMAGH

DOWN

Occupation, 1956

Agriculture   Commercial   Professional   Industrial   Others

Percentages

BELFAST   DERRY CITY   CO. ANTRIM   CO. DOWN   CO. ARMAGH   CO. DERRY   CO. TYRONE   CO. FERMANAGH

The '60s: Economic and Social Change

A MAJOR DEPARTURE in economic policy in the Republic occurred with the publication in 1958 of the Programme for Economic Expansion. This report (which was followed by two more ambitious programmes) advocated the abandonment of self-sufficiency in favour of an economic policy based on free trade, with the emphasis now on increased exports and the attraction of foreign investment into Ireland.

Above: Jack Lynch (Taoiseach 1966–73, 1977–79) signing the treaty of accession to the European Economic Community on behalf of the Republic of Ireland in 1973.

In economic terms the new policy proved very successful, with output and employment reaching levels never before recorded in the history of the state, although both small farmers and those employed in the old 'protected' industries did not share equally in the new prosperity. Emigration fell and a substantial number of those who had left in the 1950s now returned to the country. People started to marry at an earlier age than theretofore, and the birth rate began to fall.

Not surprisingly these economic and demographic changes heralded new patterns of social development. Perhaps the most important was the establishment in 1961 of a national television station, Radio Telefís Éireann, which provided a forum for social and political debate hitherto rather lacking. Evidence of new thinking was also evident in religious practice building on the deliberations of the Second Vatican Council; in educational policy, with the introduction of free secondary education; in the area of gender relations, with new opportunities opening up for Irish women; in the field of popular culture, with exposure to new styles of music, literature and art, frequently imported from Britain and America and less subject to stultifying censorship; and in the party political field, with a new emphasis upon technocratic management at the expense of old-style nationalist rhetoric.

Not everything had changed, however, and not all change was progressive: the new materialist ethos inevitably meant that those on the margins of Irish society could not fully share in the new-found wealth. Many of the 'gains' of the period proved rather ephemeral, particularly when the international economic climate turned sour in the 1970s. That said, the 1960s were characterized by a social dynamic, which, while not revolutionary, was certainly a welcome change from the atrophied atmosphere of the 1950s. The decision to enter the EEC, overwhelmingly endorsed by popular referendum in 1973, seemed to symbolize this new era although such support was undoubtedly more the result of rational economic self-interest than any new-found interest in wider European affairs.

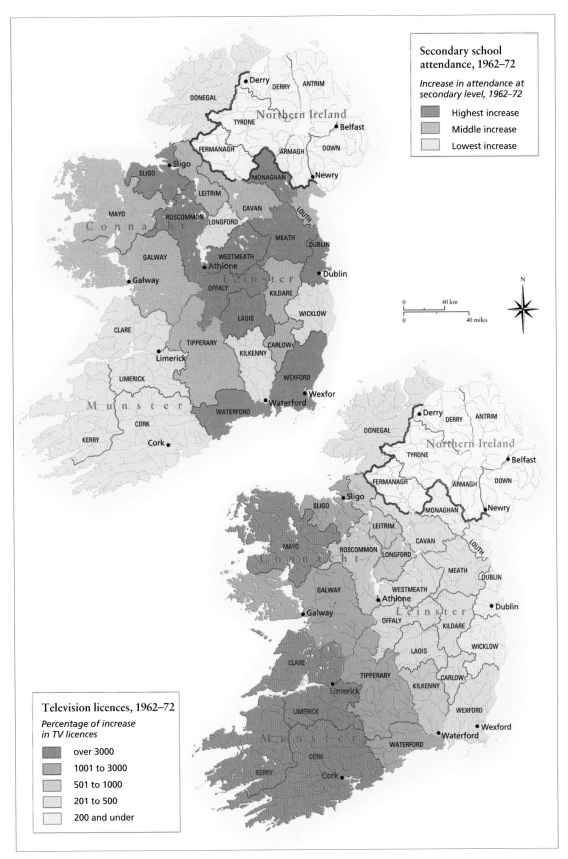

Secondary school attendance, 1962–72

Increase in attendance at secondary level, 1962–72

- Highest increase
- Middle increase
- Lowest increase

Television licences, 1962–72

Percentage of increase in TV licences

- over 3000
- 1001 to 3000
- 501 to 1000
- 201 to 500
- 200 and under

The '70s and '80s: Political and Social Instability

The expansionist economic policy heralded by the First Economic Programme was dependent on a benign international trading environment, and for most of the next 15 years such was indeed the case. When this basis was destroyed by the 'stagflation' (high inflation accompanied by increasing unemployment) which afflicted most developed economies following the oil price rise of 1973, the country was plunged once more into severe economic difficulties. Over the next 15 years, through a combination of a series of international depressions, massive government borrowing, and a decline in the financial assistance forthcoming from the European Community (which affected rural areas particularly badly) the country experienced economic turmoil which threatened to undermine the progress made in the 1960s.

Such instability was evident in the political as well as the economic field. Having experienced 15 years of uninterrupted Fianna Fáil government between 1958 and 1973 the country now experienced a series of coalitions and short-term minority administrations (with the exception of the landslide Fianna Fáil victory of 1977, which was to be tarnished within two years by a series of internal disputes), with seven General Elections being held between 1973 and 1989.

The 1980s also witnessed a new style of political debate in the country, focused in particular on the provisions of the 1937 Constitution and which saw bitterly-contested referenda in 1983 (on the issue of abortion) and 1986 (on the issue of divorce). A host of new political issues also came to the fore, particularly with regard to the quality of the environment and the provision of local services. Few administrations devised satisfactory long-term solutions to these thorny problems, and a resurgence in emigration in the late 1980s bore eloquent testimony to the sense of crisis within the Irish body politic.

It was not all doom and gloom, however, and a number of developments in the sporting and cultural fields highlighted the latent potential beneath the political stalemate. The international acclaim earned by a series of Irish authors, playwrights and musicians was mirrored by a number of sporting successes, perhaps most notably the achievements of the national football team in reaching the finals of the European Championships in Germany in 1988 and the World Cup in Italy in 1990, events which gave rise to massive, spontaneous outpourings of national pride.

Divorce Referendum, 1986

Level of support

- Highest
- Middle
- Lowest

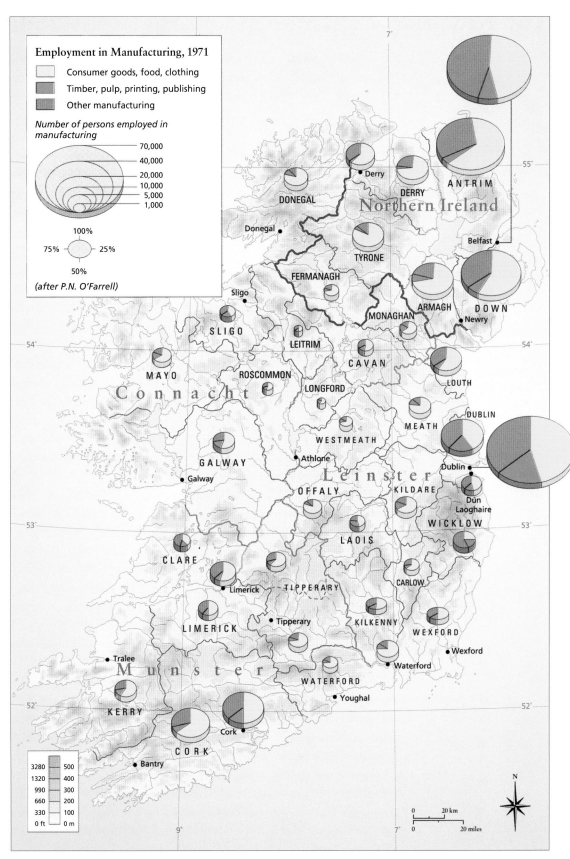

Employment in Manufacturing, 1971

- Consumer goods, food, clothing
- Timber, pulp, printing, publishing
- Other manufacturing

Number of persons employed in manufacturing

70,000
40,000
20,000
10,000
5,000
1,000

100%
75% 25%
50%

(after P.N. O'Farrell)

The Northern Crisis

Above: *Margaret Thatcher and Garret FitzGerald, whose governments negotiated the Anglo-Irish Agreement of 1985 which gave Dublin an input into the affairs of Northern Ireland, much to the fury of unionists.*

The 1960s were a decade of frustrated hope for Northern Ireland. Beginning with the promise of a new era based on improved economic performance and greater harmony between the Catholic and Protestant communities, these policies, associated with Captain Terence O'Neill, who was appointed Prime Minister in 1963, foundered on the rocks of social and political intransigence.

The frequent confrontations between Catholic Civil Rights demonstrators and Protestant opponents produced an increasingly tense atmosphere which erupted into open communal violence in 1969, in which year the British Army was deployed in Northern Ireland in an effort to restore calm.

Unfortunately, as a consequence of such mis-judged policies as the Falls Road curfew and internment without trial, the opposite occurred and the six counties experienced a spiral of violence which culminated in 1972 with an orgy of shootings and bombings unparalleled since the violence of 1922–23. Particularly prominent in these disturbances was a number of paramilitary groupings, most notably the Provisional IRA (an extreme republican organization) and the Ulster Defence Association (an equally ruthless loyalist force).

In an effort to deal with the deteriorating situation the British government prorogued Stormont and commenced 'direct rule' from Westminster. A series of initiatives followed — the Sunningdale Agreement (1973), the Power Sharing Executive (1974), the 'Rolling Devolution' plan of the early 1980s — each of which acknowledged the complexity of the situation but none of which could command cross-community support. The Anglo-Irish Agreement of 1985 institutionalized the recognition accorded by the British government to the legitimate interest of the Irish government in Northern Ireland, but notwithstanding such intermittent progress the violence associated with the unrest continued, with deaths from 'the Troubles' eventually exceeding 3,000.

A major breakthrough occurred in 1993, when the British government, via the Downing Street Declaration, explicitly recognised the right of the Irish people to self-determination (the exercise of which right was linked to consent in Northern Ireland), and the calling of cease-fires by both republican and loyalist paramilitary groups in the following year added momentum to this Irish 'peace process'. While the temporary resumption of the PIRA campaign in February 1996 delayed progress, fresh impetus was added by the subsequent election of a new, secure Labour government in London. Enthusiastic backing from the Clinton administration in Washington, allied to a renewed PIRA ceasefire, created the context for multi-party talks which produced the Good Friday Agreement of 1998.

The Northern Crisis

1. October 1968: Civil Rights march conflicts with police
2. January 1969: march attacked
3. August 1969: British troops deployed
4. July 1970: Falls Road curfew
5. August 1971: Internment swoop
6. January 1972: 'Bloody Sunday'
7. July 1972: 'Bloody Friday'
8. May 1974: Car bomb
9. January 1976: 10 workmen shot dead
10. August 1976: Peace People movement starts
11. 1978: 'Dirty protest' by prisoners
12. August 1979: 18 paratroopers killed in explosion
13. August 1979: Lord Mountbatten assassinated
14. 1980–81: hunger strikes
15. 1982: 17 people killed in bombing
16. November 1985: Anglo-Irish Agreement signed
17. May 1987: 8 IRA members shot
18. November 1987: 11 killed at War Memorial bombing
19. January 1992: 8 killed in IRA bombing
20. October 1993: Shankill Road bombing
21. October 1993: Grey Steel shootings by Loyalists
22. 1995–98: Orangemen march on Drumcree

Seats Won at the General Election, 1997

- United Kingdom Unionist
- Ulster Unionist Party
- Social Democratic and Labour Party
- Democratic Unionist Party
- Sinn Féin

The Good Friday Agreement

The Taoiseach Bertie Ahern (left), US Senator George Mitchell (centre) and British Prime Minister Tony Blair, smiling after they signed the historic Belfast Agreement on Good Friday 1998. (© PA/PA Archive/Press Association Images)

The scope and vision of the Good Friday (or Belfast) Agreement fully justified the energy expended in its negotiation. As it was popularly understood, the Agreement encompassed both a negotiated deal between most (though not all) of the local parties in Northern Ireland, and an inter-governmental accord to succeed the Anglo-Irish Agreement of 1985. It proposed actions across the three strands of the fundamental problem, and also addressed long-running sores in the local body politic, most notably by means of the creation of a new Police Service of Northern Ireland, whose impartial professionalism was ultimately to win the confidence of local Catholics to a degree that had always eluded its predecessor, the Royal Ulster Constabulary. Additional provisions, covering such diverse matters as human rights, prisoner releases and cultural issues, confirmed the status of the Agreement as a landmark in modern Irish history. The legacy of decades of mistrust between the protagonists, however, meant that its implementation proved as time-consuming and frustrating as its negotiation. The major public stumbling block was ostensibly the decommissioning of paramilitary weapons, regarding which the text of the Agreement was purposefully ambiguous, but the real nub of the matter was a society whose entrenched sectional antipathies were not amenable to swift amelioration. That one of the most bitter critics of the peace process (the proverbially oppositional Democratic Unionist Party) rapidly became the largest political grouping on the unionist side of the political fence (a process mirrored by the rise of Provisional Sinn Féin amongst northern nationalists) both exemplified this enduring communal divide, and, paradoxically, provided the means by which its worst effects could be temporised, once the decommissioning issue had largely been resolved by PIRA's actions to this end in September 2005. Thus the most distinctive feature of the new agreement concluded at St Andrews in Scotland, in October 2007, which served to complement the Good Friday accord, was, simply, the fact that the DUP was one of the signatories.

The consequent formation of a new power-sharing executive in the jurisdiction, jointly headed by two polarising veterans of the Troubles (the bellicose evangelical Protestant cleric Ian Paisley and the former PIRA figure Martin McGuinness) was an initial public success precisely because of the union of opposites their partnership signified — but understandable doubts about the long-term viability of such enforced coalition resurfaced periodically thereafter. To this day they remain a troubling counter-current to the slow incremental advance of politics in a region where history has, to paraphrase Seamus Heaney, more frequently mocked hope than rhymed with it.

Share of the Vote in Northern Ireland Assembly Elections of 1998, 2003 and 2007

APNI	Alliance Party of Northern Ireland	SDLP	Social Democratic and Labour Party
DUP	Democratic Unionist Party	SF	Sinn Féin
NIWC	Northern Ireland Women's Coalition	UKUP	United Kingdom Unionist Party
PUP	Progressive Unionist Party	UUP	Ulster Unionist Party

1998 Vote

DUP – 18.1%
UUP – 21.3%
SF – 17.6%
SDLP – 22.0%
APNI – 6.5%
UKUP – 4.5%
PUP – 2.5%
NIWC – 2.0%
Independent and others – 7.5%

2003 Vote

DUP – 25.7%
UUP – 22.7%
SF – 23.5%
SDLP – 17.0%
APNI – 3.7%
UKUP – 0.8%
PUP – 1.2%
Independent and others – 5.5%

2007 Vote

DUP – 30.1%
UUP – 14.9%
SF – 26.2%
SDLP – 15.2%
APNI – 5.2%
PUP – 0.6%
Green Party – 1.7%
Independent and others – 6.0%

The Celtic Tiger

The unfinished Anglo Irish Bank headquarters in Dublin docklands, the most conspicuous casualty of the construction bust at the end of the Celtic Tiger. The bank itself suffered the biggest corporate failure in Irish business history following years of reckless trading.
(Courtesy of Tony Kidd)

For a decade and a half, from the middle of the 1990s, Ireland experienced rapid economic growth on a scale rarely seen in any country, let alone one which had had such a poor record in the field since independence. The causes of this 'Celtic Tiger' economy were numerous, its manifestations generally (though not universally) welcome, and its social consequences profound.

Many factors — some under the control of governments of the day, others not — combined to produce this growth. Among the more important international factors that worked in Ireland's favour during this period were the global expansion of the technology sector; the creation of a European single market in the early 1990s; continuing financial support from the European Union; and the move towards a single European currency (which led to the general reduction of interest rates across the continent and the creation of the Euro later in the decade). Domestic considerations included the Northern Ireland peace process (which engendered a more favourable international opinion of the island); favourable demographic shifts (in particular the large numbers of young people entering the workplace, and the relatively small proportion of the aged); a highly educated workforce; the responsible management of state finances after 1987 (based on cross-party political consensus, and social partnership with trades unions and business); and a massive level of overseas investment (attracted in particular by the state's low level of corporate tax rates).

Evidence of this economic vitality abounded, in the form of impressive annual growth rates (reaching double figures at one point), increases in personal income (the consequence both of higher wages and lower taxes), sustained falls in unemployment, low levels of inflation, and massive surpluses on the state's balance of trade. In more human terms the period saw a growth in personal consumption, including all manner of consumer goods, foreign holidays, cars (predictably producing gridlock in many towns and cities) and, most importantly, houses. This housing boom was at once blessing and curse (it was one of the major driving forces of the growth in the latter years of the 'Tiger' era, but left many workers with a mortgaged future), and was one of the first, and worst, domestic casualties of the subsequent global economic downturn.

The influence of Ireland's economic miracle was also felt in social terms. The most important was a rapid growth in population (from 3.5 million in 1991 to 4.2 million in 2006), and, secondly, a level of immigration into Ireland unseen since the seventeenth century. These new immigrants came from numerous lands, with many in particular drawn by the lure of higher wages from the states of eastern Europe that acceded to membership of the European Union in 2004.

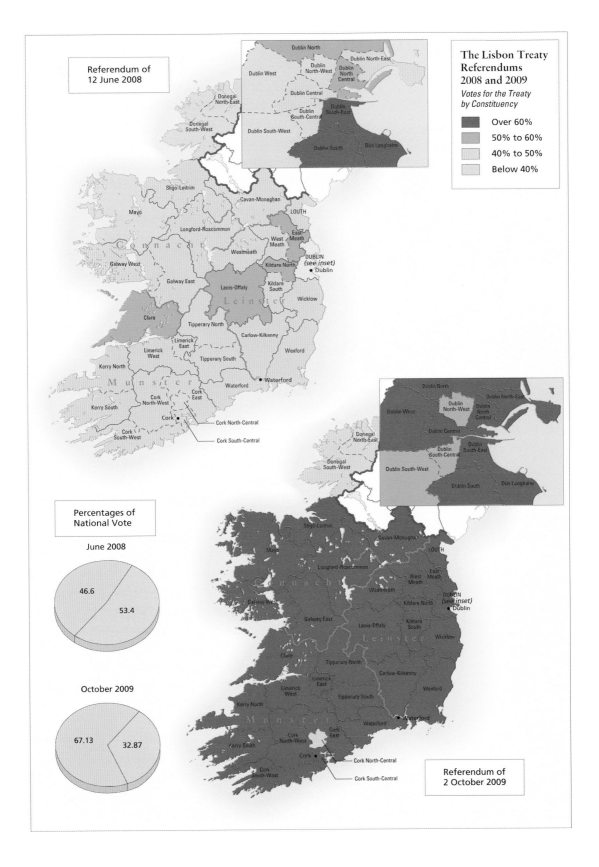

Referendum of
12 June 2008

The Lisbon Treaty
Referendums
2008 and 2009
*Votes for the Treaty
by Constituency*

Over 60%
50% to 60%
40% to 50%
Below 40%

Percentages of
National Vote

June 2008

46.6   53.4

October 2009

67.13   32.87

Referendum of
2 October 2009

Ireland: Beyond the New Millenium

Queen Elizabeth II and President Mary McAleese walk through the grounds of the Irish War Memorial Garden, Islandbridge, Dublin, during the Queen's state visit to Ireland, 2011. (© Maxwells/PA Wire)

For many reasons (including the open nature of its economy, and the inflated domestic property market) the global economic downturn of 2008 hit Ireland particularly hard, and was marked by a rapid rise in unemployment, a sharp deterioration in the state's finances, and the near collapse of the national banking structure. The popular mood was darkened still further over the following two years by a number of depressing developments including the re-emergence of emigration, and ever-more shocking revelations regarding the incidence, and cover-up, of historic abuse of minors perpetrated by members of the institutional Catholic Church. Coming hard on the heels of the confidence of the Celtic Tiger era, such setbacks were keenly felt.

It was not all bad news, however, and, as so often happens, sport provided an antidote to social malaise. During these years the achievements of two teams in particular stood out as expressions of an enduring capacity for excellence (and in so doing suggested intriguing comparisons to the depressed days of the 1940s). The Irish rugby team, in winning the Grand Slam in the Six Nations championship of 2009, performed a feat achieved by an Irish side only once before, by their predecessors of 1948, while the Kilkenny hurlers of the same year completed a four-in-a-row series of All-Ireland titles not seen since the 1941–44 Cork side, inspired by the immortal Christy Ring.

There were other straws in the wind which suggested that the future would, once again, be a dynamic one. Interestingly, history itself provided one such opening for constructive forward thinking, as plans were laid north and south of the border to mark the centenary of the historic decade from 1912 to 1923. While the fruits of these labours lie, as yet, in the history not yet made, the opportunity to go back to first principles, to measure contemporary society against the standards laid down during that decade by the 'founding fathers' of the modern republican and unionist traditions (standards which were, of course, by no means beyond reproach) may, perhaps, mark yet another turning point in the evolution of this historic nation.

This rediscovery of the past as a means of pointing the way for the future is, of course, a recurring theme in modern Irish history. It was cogently encapsulated by President Mary McAleese, during a widely-praised speech in Cork to mark the ninetieth anniversary of the Easter Rising. In the most memorable phrase of that address, she stated, proudly, that the nation was where the freedoms derived from that historic event had brought it. Where that freedom, and the legacy of history, will take it next is, as yet, unclear.

Further Reading

Aalen, F.H.A., Kevin Whelan & Matthew Stout (eds), *Atlas of the Irish Rural Landscape*, Cork University Press, 1997.

Andrews, J.H., *Ireland in Maps*, Dolmen Press, 1961.

Bagwell, Richard, *Ireland Under the Tudors*, Longman, 1885–90. *Ireland Under the Stuarts*, Longman, 1909–16.

Bardon, Jonathan, *A History of Ulster*, Blackstaff, 1992. *A History of Ireland in 250 Episodes*, Gill & Macmillan, 2008.

Barnard, T.C., *Cromwellian Ireland: English Government and Reform in Ireland, 1649–60*, Clarendon Press, 1975.

Barnard, Toby, *A New Anatomy of Ireland: the Irish Protestants, 1649–1770*, Yale University Press, 2003.

Bartlett, Thomas, *Ireland: a history*, Cambridge University Press, 2010.

Bartlett, Thomas and Keith Jeffrey (eds), *A Military History of Ireland*, Cambridge University Press, 1996.

Bew, Paul, *Ireland: the politics of enmity, 1789–2006*, Oxford University Press, 2007.

Boyce, D. George, *Nineteenth-Century Ireland: the search for stability*, Gill & Macmillan, 2005.

Bradshaw, Brendan, *The Irish Constitutional Revolution of the Sixteenth Century*, Cambridge University Press, 1979.

Brown, Terence, *Ireland: a Social and Cultural History, 1922–79*, Fontana, 1981.

Byrne, F.J., *Irish Kings and High-Kings*, Batsford, 1973.

Canny, Nicholas P., *The Elizabethan Conquest of Ireland: A Pattern Established, 1565–76*, Harvester Press, 1976. *Making Ireland British, 1580–1650*, Oxford University Press, 2001.

Comerford, R.V., *Ireland: Inventing the Nation*, Arnold, 2003.

Connolly, S.J., *Religion, Law and Power: the making of Protestant Ireland, 1660–1760*, Oxford University Press, 1992. *Contested Island: Ireland 1460–1630*, Oxford University Press, 2005.

Corish, Patrick, *The Irish Catholic Experience: a historical survey*, Gill & Macmillan, 1985.

de Paor, Máire and Liam, *Early Christian Ireland*, Thames & Hudson, 1978.

Duffy, Seán, *Ireland in the Middle Ages*, Gill & Macmillan, 1997.

Ellis, Steven G., *Tudor Ireland: Crown, Community and the Conflict of Cultures, 1470–1603*, Longman, 1985.

Foster, R.F., *Modern Ireland, 1600–1972*, Penguin, 1988. (ed) *The Oxford Illustrated History of Ireland*, Oxford University Press, 1989.

Gahan, Daniel, *The People's Rising: Wexford 1798*, Gill & Macmillan, 1995.

Gillespie, Raymond, *Seventeenth-Century Ireland: making Ireland modern*, Gill & Macmillan, 2006.

Harbison, Peter, *Pre Christian Ireland*, Thames & Hudson, 1988. (ed) *The Shell Guide to Ireland*, Macmillan, 1989.

Hennessey, Thomas, *A History of Northern Ireland, 1920–1996*, Gill & Macmillan, 1997.

Jackson, Alvin, *Ireland 1798–1998*, Wiley-Blackwell, 1999.

Kelly, James, *Prelude to Union: Anglo-Irish Politics in the 1780s*, Cork University Press, 1992.

Keogh, Dermot, *Twentieth-Century Ireland: nation and state*, Gill & Macmillan, 2005.

Kinealy, Christine, *This Great Calamity, The Irish Famine, 1845–52*, Gill & Macmillan, 1994.

Lee, Joseph, *Ireland, 1912–85*, Cork University Press, 1989.

Lennon, Colm, *Sixteenth-Century Ireland*, Gill & Macmillan, 1994.

Lydon, James, *The Lordship of Ireland in the Middle Ages*, Gill & Macmillan, 1972.

Lyons, F.S.L. (ed), *Ireland since the Famine*, Fontana, 1973.

McBride, Ian, *Eighteenth-Century Ireland: the isle of slaves*, Gill & Macmillan, 2009.

McCavitt, John, *The Flight of the Earls*, Gill & Macmillan, 2002.

Meehan, Bernard, *The Book of Kells*, Thames & Hudson, 1994.

Mitchell, Frank, *The Shell Guide to Reading the Irish Landscape*, Country House, 1986.

Morgan, Hiram, *Tyrone's Rebellion: The outbreak of the Nine Years War in Tudor Ireland*, Gill & Macmillan, 1993.

Ó Corráin, Donncha, *Ireland before the Normans*, Gill & Macmillan, 1972.

Ó Siochrú, Micheál, *God's Executioner: Oliver Cromwell and the conquest of Ireland*, Faber and Faber, 2008.

O'Kelly, M.J., *Early Ireland*, Cambridge University Press, 1989.

Stalley, Roger, *The Cistercian Monasteries of Ireland*, Yale University Press, 1987.

Townshend, Charles, *Easter 1916: the Irish rebellion*, Allen Lane, 2005.

Index

References in this index in **bold** face are for maps or pictures

Acknowledgements

THE PUBLISHERS would like to thank to following for the photographs and illustrations produced in this atlas:

Peter Newark's Historical Pictures, Bath, England: 14, 24, 26, 28, 35, 50, 52, 53, 56, 60, 62, 64, 66, 68, 71, 73, 78, 82, 90, 92, 94, 96, 102.
Other photographs and illustrations:
Con Brogan
Industrial Development Agency of Ireland
National Gallery of Ireland
National Library of Ireland
National Museum of Ireland
Private Collections
Trinity College, Dublin

For Arcadia Editions Limited:

Design and Cartography: Peter Gamble
Elsa Gibert
Isabelle Lewis
Jeanne Radford
Malcolm Swanston
Jonathan Young

Editorial: Shirley Ellis
Andrew Lavender
Elizabeth Wyse

Illustration: Peter Massey
Peter Smith

Typesetting: Jeanne Radford